What people are saying about
STOP WATCHING, START DOING ...

"This book is going to be a big hit. I know it!"
—Bob Goff, New York Times Best-Selling Author of *Love Does* and Founder of *Restore International*

"I can't say enough about E.J. Swanson. When I first met him, I was impressed with a man who knew who he was in Christ and was willing to learn from others, so he could be more like Jesus in his marriage, ministry, and community. I've watched E.J. help thousands of teens understand who they are in Christ and how to live deeply in His story. *Stop Watching, Start Doing* is not only a call to live beyond being a consumer, but a practical guide to accomplishing all that God created you to be."
—Mark Matlock, President of *Youth Specialties* and Founder of the *Planet Wisdom* student conferences

"EJ has this innate ability to pull at the hearts of today's teens by awakening them to experience the heart of God. This book makes a compelling case for why every student must be a part of an energizing Kingdom vision that is worthy of sacrifice and pursuit."
—Jeremy Zach, Student Specialist for *XP3 Orange*

"E.J. and Robert have brought together years of experience in speaking and Biblical teaching with a book that both inspires and gives practical wisdom for bringing faith to life and making a difference in the world. You guys have nailed it!"
—Eric Woods, Retreats Director, *Springhill Camps*

"This is an absolutely incredible tool for anyone ready to be a Kingdom worker, but needs the next steps. This book has the potential to launch a movement! Not only will I give it to the students in my church, I can't wait to have my own kids read it!"
—Jason Raitz, Speaker & Church Planter

"E.J. Swanson and Robert Noland want to help you live a better life—one that involves getting your hands dirty and taking an active role in where you want to go. They've helped thousands of people do this—and you'll be better, because you took the time to learn from them!"
—Matt Brown, evangelist, author, and founder of *Think Eternity*

ABOUT THE AUTHORS . . .

E. J. SWANSON

As a nationally known communicator, E.J. Swanson's commitment to expressing the reality of Christ sets the stage for his exciting and compelling message to audiences of all ages. Focusing on the Christ-centered truth of God's Word, E.J.'s energetic personality provides an exceptional ability to communicate in a way that is, not only engaging and fun, but challenging and inspiring as well.

E.J. is the founder of *I Won't Watch*—iwontwatch.com, the inspiration for the *Stop Watching, Start Doing* book. *IWW* has given millions of dollars to some of the most globally impacting ministries on the planet, serving the millions of impoverished and hurting people around the world today. E.J. lives in Troy, Michigan with his lovely bride, Abbey.

ROBERT NOLAND

Robert began his writing career as a songwriter, while touring for 10 years in Christian music. He released his first series of Bible studies in 1988 and in 1991 began writing for a para-church student ministry. Noland has since authored over 40 titles spanning from children to adult audiences for denominations, faith-based organizations, and Christian ministries. Robert's first book entitled *The Knight's Code* was released in 2010. He launched a men's web site—theknightscode.com—and speaks regularly at men's events. Robert is now a free-lance writer, living in Franklin, Tennessee with his wife of 30 years, and has two grown sons.

SPECIAL THANKS

From E.J—This book is dedicated to my bride and best friend, Abbey! May we live out Micah 6:8 and together do justice, love kindness, and always walk humbly with God!

From Robert—For Jesus, Robin, Rhett & Rheed—my motivation for "doing" every day. To E.J. for partnering in this labor of God's love.

From E.J. & Robert—To Scott & Amy for turning text into art.

STOP WATCHING START DOING

A REALITY CHECK TO ACTIVATE YOUR FAITH

E.J. SWANSON
WITH ROBERT NOLAND

Recommended Applications for
Stop Watching, Start Doing

- Read for yourself to challenge and inspire your walk with God.
- Read, discuss, and process in a group of peers.
- Read and lead to disciple a group of younger believers.
- Read and lead with your family.
- Any small group, Sunday school, or discipleship setting.

Discussion questions are at the end of each chapter of the book.

Stop Watching, Start Doing
Published by The Ministry Collective, Inc.
Troy, MI 48083
In Cooperation with
517 Resources, Inc.
Franklin, TN 37064

Copyright © 2013 E.J. Swanson
Copyright © 2013 Robert Noland
Created in the U.S.A 2013

Cover Design: Scott Burks for Fishhouse Creative
Interior Design: Amy Balamut

ISBN: 978-0-9829130-9-3

NLV© Christian Literature International / Scripture taken from the HOLY BIBLE, NEW INTERNATIONAL VERSION®. Copyright © 1973, 1978, 1984 Biblica. Used by permission of Zondervan. All rights reserved. / Scripture taken from The Message. Copyright © 1993, 1994, 1995, 1996, 2000, 2001, 2002. Used by permission of NavPress Publishing Group. / Contemporary English Version® Copyright © 1995 American Bible Society. All rights reserved. / Scripture quotations marked NLT are taken from the Holy Bible, New Living Translation, copyright 1996, 2004. Used by permission of Tyndale House Publishers, Inc., Wheaton, Illinois 60189. All rights reserved. / Good News Translation® (Today's English Version, Second Edition) Copyright © 1992 American Bible Society. All rights reserved.

For more information, visit
ejswanson.org & www.iwontwatch.com

CONTENTS

CHAPTER 1 — WHY AM I HERE? 7

CHAPTER 2 — WHO ARE YOU GOING TO BE? 20

CHAPTER 3 — SO, WHAT IS YOUR GIFT? 31

CHAPTER 4 — SO, WHAT'S STOPPING YOU? 48

CHAPTER 5 — WHAT NEED IN THE WORLD MATCHES YOUR GIFT? ... 62

CHAPTER 6 — CAN YOU STOP WATCHING? 72

CHAPTER 7 — WILL YOU LIVE OUT YOUR CALLING? 88

CHAPTER 8 — WILL YOU THINK LIKE A DO-ER 99

CHAPTER 9 — WILL YOU ACT LIKE A DO-ER? 109

CHAPTER 10 — WILL YOU START DOING? 128

CHAPTER 1

WHY AM I HERE?

If you've picked up this book to read, there's a strong likelihood you're a Christ-follower. If that's the case, the time you take to read this book is going to be a healthy investment in your future.

If you're not a Christian, we're really glad you have this in your hands and we're going to ask you to be open-minded as you search for truth in these pages. Consider that, if what we say here turns out to be true, you stand to gain a lot by taking this experience in and practicing the principles given here. If, by this book's end, you aren't convinced, then you've at least searched out Christianity for yourself and can check another belief system off your list. But, we're banking on you finding your life in these pages. Hang with us. Stay open. Read on.

THE UNLIVED LIFE

"Why am I here?" A question everyone asks—often. The incredible thing is that it has already been answered. Maybe not in the way most of us would like, but it is answered.

A dad's little daughter had just learned a new phrase, but didn't quite understand it yet, as kids often tend to do. She toddled over to him and asked, "Daddy, what are you doing in the world?" An obvious twist of "What in the world are you doing?" He said it really made him think, "What *am* I doing in the world?!"

In the Disney movie, *Tuck Everlasting*, a family discovers the fountain of youth. They have become eternal beings, forever locked into the age that they first drank the water. A young lady named Winnie, who has befriended the family, discovers their secret and wants to drink from the water too. The father tells her, "If there's one thing I've learned about people, it's that they will do anything—anything—not to die. And they'll do anything to keep from living their life. What we Tucks have, you can't call it living. We just are. We're like rocks, stuck at the side of a stream. Don't be afraid of death, Winnie. Be afraid of the unlived life."

To consider why we are here and what life we must live, we should first realize there is a beginning—birth—and an end—death. The end is what makes the life so valuable and crucial. We don't know how much time we have. Every day, any day, could be the last. We just don't know. This creates an urgency that few embrace; in fact, most ignore.

When we're young, it is really easy to live like we have 60-70 years ahead of us and statistics prove that *may* be true. But, still, no one knows. We assume we're the exception. But this is also why when a young person dies tragically; it is so devastating to family, friends, and the community. It drives home the reality of a short-lived life.

A wise man once said, "On every grave stone is a birth year and a death year, and then there's a little dash in between. It's the dash that counts."

So, it is a strong possibility that you are searching with us all for why you are here. What is your purpose? Is there a grand plan that you are part of? We wrote this book to say, "YES! Absolutely!" but we also want to explain how you can find *your* plan.

THE HOLE IN OUR SOULS

There is a foundational element to discovering your purpose. Without this Cornerstone of your life, there is no reason to move forward, to explore any other thought. If you have already made this life choice before, we encourage you to read it again here. Each time you hear it, helps ground you in your faith.

Here we go ...

Before we can discuss the state of mankind, we have to take a look at our personal worldview. What each of us believes about the origin of life is crucial to what we believe about ourselves. How so? Well, simply put, your belief in how man came to existence is crucial to faith. A person who believes we morphed from monkeys or grew legs and arms from a batch of primordial ooze is going to have trouble believing life has much purpose and meaning. The truth is we are no cosmic accident. We are designed and made by a loving Father Who has a plan for each of us. Believing you were created out of a deep love—to both love and be loved—gives hope and meaning to life.

"For you created my inmost being; you knit me together in my mother's womb. I praise you because I am fearfully and wonderfully made..." (Psalm 139:13–14a, NIV)

Who knows more about a creation than its Creator? Only God can make a person, and then also, make a person new. Starting with Adam and Eve and their choice to listen to God's enemy and to disobey, we also are born with this condition called sin. We continue it with our own choices. No one had to teach us to lie, steal, cheat, have bad attitudes, scream when we don't get our way, and on and on. That is inherent in who we are—to love ourselves and care for our own needs above anyone else. Sin is disobedience to God's ways and choosing our own path. We are all guilty as charged.

This has caused a God-shaped hole in our soul, an emptiness or void inside each of us. We all try to fill this hole in our own way—with a sport, talent, relationship, or by pretending to be someone or something we're not. We can try to fill it with drugs, alcohol, illicit sex, materialism, or other unhealthy habits. We can try to stuff our soul with a lot of things, but none of them will give us real peace. Even if we try really hard to be morally good, we still do things that are not pleasing to God. We cannot see on our own that God is the answer to our emptiness; His Spirit has to help us see that. Listen to Paul's words expressing his own frustration . . .

> We know that the Law is right and good, but I am a person who does what is wrong and bad. I am not my own boss. Sin is my boss. I do not understand myself. I want to do what is right but I do not do it. Instead, I do the very thing I hate. When I do the thing I do not want to do, it shows me that the Law is right and good. So I am not doing it. Sin living in me is doing it. I know there is nothing good in me, that is, in my flesh. For I want to do good but I do not. I do not do the good I want to do. Instead, I am always doing the sinful things I do not want to do. If I am always doing the very thing I do not want to do, it means I am no longer the one who does it. It is sin that lives in me. This has become my way of life: When I want to do what is right, I always do what is wrong. My mind and heart agree with the Law of God. But there is a different law at work deep inside of me that fights with my mind. This law of sin holds me in its power because sin is still in me. There is no happiness in me! Who can set me free from my sinful old self? (Romans 7:14–24, NLV)

The Bible defines sin as attitudes, thoughts, motives, and actions that displease God. Every person since Adam and Eve has had this problem. The Bible says, *". . . righteousness from God comes through faith in Jesus Christ to all who believe. There is no difference, for all have sinned and fall short of the glory of God, and are justified freely by his grace through the redemption that came by Christ Jesus."* (Romans 3:22–24, NIV)

Here's our quick summary of this passage—God will give you His righteousness, if you choose to receive it. Everyone has blown it eternally. But God's grace will redeem us and correct the shortfall.

In John 14:5b-6 Thomas asked Jesus, *"Lord, how can we know the way?"* Jesus answered, *"I am the way and the truth and the life. No one comes to the Father except through me."*

Born with the same nature as Adam and Eve, we have decided to disobey God as they did (Genesis 3, Romans 17:15-20). To be saved before a holy God, we need His power (Romans 8:8). John 3:16-17 (MSG) says, *"This is how much God loved the world: he gave his Son, his one and only Son. And this is why: so that no one need be destroyed; by believing in him, anyone can have a whole and lasting life. God didn't go to all the trouble of sending his Son merely to point an accusing finger, telling the world how bad it was. He came to help, to put the world right again."*

The Bible says the price for sin is death, which means separation from God (Romans 6:23). Because God is holy, He requires punishment by death for the choices we have made. Jesus came to give Himself as the final sacrifice for us (Hebrews 7:27). No more lambs are slaughtered on altars to atone for sin, because the Sacrificial Lamb of God shed His blood once and for all.

> *"For you know that it was not with perishable things such as silver or gold that you were redeemed from the empty way of life handed down to you from your forefathers, but with the precious blood of Christ, a lamb without blemish or defect. He was chosen before the creation of the world, but was revealed in these last times for your sake." (1 Peter 1:18-20, NIV)*

Jesus died, so you wouldn't have to! Christ died in your place! (Romans 5:8)

Jesus took our punishment for us. By giving His life. He proved God's great love for us. John 15:13 says, *"Greater love has no one than this, that he lay down his life for his friends."* Each person must make his/her own choice: whether or not to accept Jesus' death in place of his/her own. He loves us enough to give us free will, the choice as to whether to accept Him or not.

Romans 5:6 says, *"Christ arrives right on time to make this happen. He didn't, and doesn't, wait for us to get ready. He presented himself for this sacrificial death when we were far too weak and rebellious to do anything to get ourselves ready."* (MSG)

FOUR STEPS TO LIFE

Praying to receive Jesus Christ as your Lord and Savior is the biggest step and the best choice you will ever make. But asking Him to take control of your life is just the beginning. There is a relationship to live out every day with Him.

So, let's go through the Gospel one more time to review. We'll use four simple steps.

Step 1
Because of our sin or disobedience to God, we are separated from Him.

Step 2
Because of this separation and God's desire to provide a solution, Jesus died on the cross for our sins. They buried Him in a tomb, but then on the third day, He came alive and walked out of the grave to live forever. Jesus now sits at the right hand of God.

Step 3
Because Jesus defeated sin and death, we can now have a relationship with God right here and also secure a home in Heaven when we die.

Step 4
If we accept God's offer for salvation through faith in Christ, we are now His friend, are saved from Hell, and can live with Him in Eternity. Because He is now in our heart, we

can pray to Him, read and understand His Word, share Him with others, and be molded into His image.

If you would like to ask Jesus into your life, simply pray and ask Him. If you're ready, you can pray this prayer or use your own words:

Prayer: *Dear God, I know I am a sinner and need Your forgiveness. I now turn from my sins and ask You into my life to be my Savior and Lord. Please forgive my sins and give me Your gift of eternal life. Thank You for dying for me, saving me, and changing my life. In Jesus' name. Amen.*

If you prayed that prayer, you need to let someone know—a pastor or a trusted Christian friend. Your relationship with Jesus needs to be public, not private. We're not supposed to hide Him. We are to share Him. We're supposed to let people know and be open about the fact that He lives in our hearts.

If you have no idea who to contact—go to or call a church near you that you know is a Bible-believing, Christ-centered church. Tell them you prayed to ask Christ into your life and want someone to know. (It might be a good idea for you to bring this book and show them the prayer you prayed.) This is one of the biggest and best decisions you could ever make, so please share it with the important people in your life.

We would also be excited to hear about your decision at info@iwontwatch.com. If you have no one else to tell right now, tell us! We want to know!

If you were already a Christian, reading or hearing the Gospel again is great to remind you of who you are in Christ and what God has done for you. You want to be certain your decision is strong and you are on track in growing your relationship with Him.

Now that everyone is on the same page, let's move forward from the Cornerstone and build the building!

DEEPEST, DARKEST, DIRTIEST

Once the Gospel of Jesus Christ, coupled with the Holy Spirit of God, is alive in your soul, it begins to work its way into every area of your life, exposing the deepest, darkest, and dirtiest parts of you.

When gunk—hair, skin, etc.—the pieces of us that we shed daily—clogs up the drain pipes in our house, it can actually start to back up the water to the point where it won't drain, so we can't use the shower, tub, or sink, and we can't even get clean anymore. We have to get Drano Max, or some other clog remover, that goes down to the problem area, disintegrates the gunk, and opens the drainpipe back up, so the water flows again and we can get clean.

The things that we hide in our lives—the dirty little secrets, the nastiness of our hearts—clogs up our spirits, making us dysfunctional and unhealthy, no longer able to see, care about, or fulfill our purpose. This is why we need rescue and why we must daily keep our hearts clean by calling on the Lord to forgive us, to keep us pure and holy.

So many people respond to God by saying, "I know I need to get things right with You, but I have to get my life straightened out first. As soon as I do that, I'll come to You." That is exactly like this conversation . . .

A man tells his friend, "I had a major accident and my car isn't even drive-able anymore." His friend asks, "So are you going to take it in to a body shop to get it fixed?" "Oh no," the man answers. "I can't do that. It's way too messed up. It would be so embarrassing to face the people at the body shop and admit I had an accident. I'm going to put the car in my garage, work on it myself with a hammer, some body filler, and duct tape. When I feel like I have my car in better shape and it doesn't look so bad, I'll tow it into the body shop."

We can think that is a ridiculous scenario, but that is exactly what many people think they must do—"fix" their lives first—before giving it to God.

After you come to Christ, take all your nastiness and gunk and just lay it out there. He sees it already, He knows what is there, even better than you do, and here's the great news of the Gospel: Only God knows *exactly* what to do with it!

Jesus knows how to . . .
    help you
        rescue you
            redeem you
                heal you,
                    make you, and
mold you into an amazing instrument in His hands!

Jesus came to them and said, "I have been given all authority in heaven and on earth! Go to the people of all nations and make them my disciples. Baptize them in the name of the Father, the Son, and the Holy Spirit, and teach them to do everything I have told you. I will be with you always, even until the end of the world." (Matthew 28:18–20, CEV)

This message was for the believers of that day and every believer leading right up to you.

YOU IN? YOUR CALL.

God wants to involve you in His work. He wants your life to make a difference in thousands of other lives. He wants to empower you to

Is there something that you know you need to get rid of in your life? A thing? An activity? A relationship? You know it is hurting you and you must stop. Today—renounce it. Get help. Give it up. Tell a friend. Reach in and reach out.

move His Kingdom forward and defeat the work of the enemy. That's exactly what redemption means—taking something headed the wrong way and turning it around for good.

You were lost, but now you're found. And you're not only found, you are in His hand—forever! He will never leave you or forsake you. You still have the choice to leave Him, to forsake and renounce Him, but He's all about you now. You are so in!

John 15:5–8, Jesus says, "Yes, I am the vine; you are the branches. Those who remain in me, and I in them, will produce much fruit. For apart from me you can do nothing. Anyone who does not remain in me is thrown away like a useless branch and withers. Such branches are gathered into a pile to be burned. But if you remain in me and my words remain in you, you may ask for anything you want, and it will be granted! When you produce much fruit, you are my true disciples. This brings great glory to my Father." (NLT)

Pay attention to the last sentence in the first verse—*"For apart from me, you can do nothing."* This little verse is huge in understanding how God works. So many people ask Christ into their lives, then run off and start trying to do "good things" to impress Him and get His approval. But, know this now . . .

You are already approved!

You can do nothing without Him.

So, every day, live life with Jesus to know what you are to do and do nothing without Him!

JAMES, BONO, & YOU

People talk about their faith, go to Bible studies to grow their faith, get into deep discussions about their faith, constantly learning, waiting, yet wasting time by accomplishing nothing. Of course, we must attend Bible studies and discuss our faith, but education should always be for one thing—preparation for action.

> *Dear friends, do you think you'll get anywhere in this if you learn all the right words but never do anything? Does merely talking about faith indicate that a person really has it? For instance, you come upon an old friend dressed in rags and half-starved and say, "Good morning, friend! Be clothed in Christ! Be filled with the Holy Spirit!" and walk off without providing so much as a coat or a cup of soup—where does that get you? Isn't it obvious that God-talk without God-acts is outrageous nonsense? I can already hear one of you agreeing by saying, "Sounds good. You take care of the faith department, I'll handle the works department." Not so fast. You can no more show me your works apart from your faith than I can show you my faith apart from my works. Faith and works, works and faith, fit together hand in glove. (James 2:14–18, CEV)*

In an interview where Bono, the iconic lead singer for the rock band U2, was being asked about his faith and his many humanitarian works all around the world, he responded, "A wise man once told me, 'Stop asking God to bless what you're doing. Get involved in what God is doing, because it's already blessed.'"

So, now you should know why you're here. You're here to live for Christ, because He died for you. But now He lives in you. You and He make an amazing team that can, quite literally, change the world.

Are you ready to stop being beaten up by the culture and taken advantage of by the world? Are you ready to turn the tide, turn those tables, and turn up the heat on your life? Ready to find your purpose and go after the things of God?

ARE YOU READY TO STOP WATCHING AND START DOING?!

CHAPTER 1 DISCUSSION QUESTIONS

1. How does—or can—the understanding of death actually bring more value to life?

2. Does thinking about discovering your purpose stress you out or excite you? Explain your answer.

3. On a scale of 1 to 10—1 meaning it's not on your radar at all to 10 being it's all consuming to you, how much does finding your purpose in life matter to you?

4. Why is grasping the reality of sin, or disobedience to God, foundational in starting your faith journey? Why does it matter? How does it affect your God-concept?

5. How does, or how should, the fact that Christ died in your place affect your view of your life and purpose?

6. If you're a Christian, briefly tell how you came to know Him.

7. In the featured questions on page 15—is there anything you need to get rid of today? Would anyone like to share what you're struggling with or would you like prayer today for any need?

8. Talk about this sentence—"So, every day, live life with Jesus to know what you are to do and do nothing without Him."

9. Discuss Bono's statement—"Stop asking God to bless what you're doing. Get involved in what God is doing, because it's already blessed."

10. Do you have any question about this chapter or is there anything that you didn't understand and need clarity on?

> **POST/TWEET**
> Christ died for me. I live for Him. We make an amazing team that can, quite literally, change the world.
> #stopwatchingstartdoing

CHAPTER 2

WHO ARE YOU GOING TO BE?

This chapter is going to center around an action-packed Bible story and each of us will find ourselves inside it. Buckle up!

In 1 Samuel, chapter 14, we find Jonathan, the son of King Saul, telling his armor-bearer, "Come, let's go over to the Philistine outpost on the other side." Jonathan was with his dad and his troops outside of Gibeah. The Philistines were the enemy. Saul was taking it easy, having pitched his tent under a fruit tree. Jonathan was tired of waiting and ready for action. He wasn't in charge of the army, but he was in charge of himself and his own armor-bearer. So off they went without telling anyone.

DYNAMIC DUO

Here's the story from 1 Samuel 14, broken down in our own words...

On each side of the pass, that Jonathan intended to cross to reach the Philistine outpost, was a cliff. Jonathan said to his young armor-bearer, "Let's go. Perhaps the Lord will act in our behalf. Nothing can hinder the Lord from saving, whether by many or by few." Jonathan's main man responded, "Do all that you have in mind. Go ahead; I am with you heart and soul." Jonathan said, "Come on, then; we will cross over toward them and let them see us. If they say to us, 'Wait there until we come to you,' we will stay where we are and not go up to them. But if they say, 'Come up to us,' we will climb up, because that will be our sign that the Lord has given them into our hands."

So both of them showed themselves to the Philistine outpost. "Look!" said the Philistines. "The Hebrews are crawling out of the holes they were hiding in." The men of the outpost shouted to Jonathan and his armor-bearer, "Come up to us and we'll teach you a lesson!" So Jonathan said to his armor-bearer, "Climb up after me; the Lord has given them into the hand of Israel." (Notice he didn't say himself, but Israel.)

Jonathan climbed up, only using his hands and feet, with his armor-bearer right behind him. The Philistines fell as Jonathan advanced and his armor-bearer followed, fighting behind him. In that first attack, the two warriors killed some twenty men in an area of about half an acre.

Then panic struck the whole army—those in the camp and the field, those in the outposts and raiding parties—and the ground shook. It was a panic sent by God. Saul's lookouts at Gibeah in Benjamin saw the army melting away in all directions. Then Saul said to the men who were with him, "Muster the forces and see who has left us." When they did, it was Jonathan and his armor-bearer who were not there. Saul said to Ahijah, "Bring the ark of God." (At that time it was with the Israelites.) While Saul was talking to the priest, the chaos in the Philistine camp increased more and more. So Saul said to the priest, "Withdraw your hand." Then Saul and all his men assembled and went to the battle. They found the Philistines in total confusion, striking each other with their swords. Those Hebrews who had previously been with the Philistines and had gone up with them to their camp went over to the Israelites who were with Saul and Jonathan. When all the Israelites who had hidden in the hill country of Ephraim heard that the Philistines were on the run, they joined the battle in hot pursuit. So on that day the Lord saved Israel—using Jonathan and his armor bearer.

FRONT LINES OR SIDELINES?

Israel was being held at bay by a battalion of Philistines that controlled the pass at Mikmash. And what was the leader of Israel doing? Verse 2 states, *"Saul was staying on the outskirts of Gibeah under a pomegranate tree in Migron."*

So while an army of 600 sat waiting with their king, two men took action and defeated the enemy. Moral of this story: Two warriors + God > 600 enemy troops.

Instead of fighting on the front lines, Saul was sitting on the sidelines. And this was no isolated incident. Do you remember what Saul said to David when he offered to fight Goliath? He said, "You are only a boy." You would think a great leader would say, "You know what? If a boy is ready to go out and fight a giant for my nation, then surely I can go out and fight him! After all, I'm the king!" But Saul didn't go out to fight Goliath in place of David. He sat on the sidelines, while a shepherd boy ran to the front lines! Scripture says that Saul was head and shoulders taller than any Israelite. So the only one who matched up to Goliath physically was too cowardly or lazy to fight.

So, David that day, and Jonathan this day, goes out to the front lines. But Saul, once again, sits back and watches.

> Is there something that you know you need to do, but are waiting on someone else to take care of for you? Why are you waiting? Front lines or sidelines? Your call.

Let's change focus onto another person in the story—someone whom we don't even know his name—Jonathan's armor-bearer. Don't you love his response to Jonathan? "Go ahead. I am with you heart and soul." In other words: "I'm all in, my man! Let's do this!"

We all need armor-bearers in our lives—people who are with us heart and soul. They pray for us, believe in us, inspire us, and encourage us. And fight for us.

Here is a very important point—get this! Not all of us are supposed to be Jonathan's. Some of us are designed and blessed by God to be amazing armor-bearers. Behind-the-scenes people that are actually moving, shaking, and making things happen. We don't know how Jonathan would have managed by himself with all those Philistines, but we can safely say the armor-bearer likely cinched the victory for them. Even if he only provided 20 percent of the fight in the battle, that could have made the difference in victory or defeat, life or death, for Jonathan.

When you look realistically at Jonathan's plan, it was such a bad idea! If there are only two of you against an entire battalion of Philistines, your only hope is the element of surprise. So maybe wait until the middle of the night and then sneak up on them. But Jonathan does the exact opposite! He walks into the middle of this canyon in broad daylight and makes himself known to the enemy. "Hey! Here I am! Over here, guys!"

And then he tells the armor-bearer what he'll consider a sign from God on how to attack and if God is guaranteeing him victory: "If they say, 'Wait there until we come to you,' we will wait on them and then fight. But if they say, 'Come up to us,' then we'll take the fight to them, and not only that, then God is telling us that we'll win!"

Let's just make an observation here. . . Jonathan made up the sign. I don't know about you, but if I'm making up the signs, I would do the exact opposite. If they come down to us, that'll be our sign. In fact, if they fall off the cliff, that'll be a definite sign that we'll win!

Jonathan's plan makes no military sense. It would never be taught at West Point as a brilliant strategy. They're going to give up the high ground, while being grossly outnumbered. So the Philistines taunt them, "Look! The Hebrews are crawling out of the holes they were hiding in."

Here's the next observation . . . Have you ever done any rock climbing? Can you imagine rock climbing on a cliff, with no ropes or stakes, then having to fight for your life with a heavy sword and shield when you get to the top?! The last thing you want to do in preparation for a sword fight is climb a cliff! But that doesn't stop

Jonathan. Or his armor-bearer. They were together—heart and soul! Why would they do this? Because Jonathan had a Secret Weapon: "Perhaps the Lord will act in our behalf."

And the Secret Weapon worked—"So on that day the Lord saved Israel."

The course of Israel's history was changed by one man with the right mindset: "Perhaps the Lord will act in our behalf." What if Jonathan had sat on the sidelines like the rest of the Israelites? With his dad and king—Saul? What if the armor bearer had told Jonathan "no?"

Here's a truth we can draw from this story: If Jonathan hadn't done anything, then nothing would have happened!

That reminds us of a story...

This is the tale of four people. Their names were Everybody, Somebody, Anybody, and Nobody. There was an important job to be done and Everybody was sure that Somebody would do it. Anybody could have done it, but Nobody did it. Somebody got angry about it, because it was Everybody's job. Everybody thought that Anybody could do it, but Nobody realized that Everybody wouldn't do it. It ended up that Everybody blamed Somebody when Nobody did what Anybody could have done.

If you sit back and do nothing, you are definitely on the sidelines. And if you're on the front lines, no one has to tell you that you are; and everyone around you knows it!

FAITH + ACTION = IMPACT

Jonathan and his armor-bearer's victory wasn't about talent or intelligence, beauty or brawn. It was about faith and action.

Ever heard of nitroglycerin? It's an explosive chemical used in demolition and excavation. It can be ignited by even the slightest impact. In the 1800s, the state of California outlawed the transportation of nitroglycerin, because a crate of it destroyed a Wells Fargo office, killing 15 people. Ironically, the two primary ingredients—nitrogen and glycerin—are not dangerous at all by themselves until they are mixed together in the proper proportions and conditions. Then the combination is deadly.

In the battle against evil in this world, faith and action can be fairly harmless entities, but mixed together in the right person in the right conditions can rock the world!

So, let's do a highlights recap here . . .

Saul parked and watched, doing nothing about the war. He sat back, as he had with David and Goliath, on the sideline, and allowed Jonathan to go fight, win, and gain the glory for God.

Jonathan took the initiative by stepping out in faith and inviting his armor-bearer to join him.

In the first strike alone, they slaughtered 20 Philistines. The Lord honored their bold move by sending a panic upon the enemy, confusing the army so much that they killed each other, shaking the earth, and forcing king Saul and his 600 warriors into the battle.

Once again, the Lord miraculously saved Israel, using one man who dared to take initiative!

Jonathan had a loyal helper in his armor-bearer. Armor-bearers in ancient times had to be unusually brave and loyal, since the lives of their masters often depended on them. The armor-bearer's statement shows the extent of his great loyalty, "Go ahead. I am with you heart and soul."

While we have been focused on this particular story and passage, it is important to note that King Saul was once an anointed king chosen by God. What prompted him to lose God's favor? Poor decisions. Saul was once in the place of Jonathan, but a series of sins changed his direction and blessing.

In life, a Jonathan can be one decision away from becoming a Saul. In the Kingdom of God, however, a Saul can repent and become a Jonathan once again. And an armor bearer can advance in

God's favor and blessing to become the Jonathan. Obedience, coupled with the grace of God, can change life forever!

WHO DO YOU IDENTIFY WITH?

Throughout your life, it is likely you will find yourself being a Jonathan in situations and then an armor bearer in others. You might even find yourself having a Saul attitude in a particular circumstance. The point in this chapter is to challenge you to evaluate *over-all* which one of these people you tend to be. What tendency do you have—sidelines, leading, or supporting/serving? Determining your tendency is crucial to moving forward in your gifts.

So, whom do you *most* identify with? Saul? Jonathan? The armor-bearer?

If your answer is Saul, then you are sitting on the sidelines, watching life go by. Saul had little honor and love for God. This was evident again in this story. In fact, in verses 1–3, we hear about Ahijah, the priest for Saul. One of his jobs was to hear from God and tell Saul. This means that Saul wasn't seeking God on his own. He was relying on someone else's relationship. A definite sign of a Saul is not seeking God for oneself.

If your answer is Jonathan, then you mix faith with action. You want to be a part of God's Kingdom coming here on earth. Being His ambassador and changing the world—one heart at a time. You are ready and willing to go into battle and lead others.

If you are an armor-bearer, then you are willing to say to the Jonathans of the world, "Go ahead. I am with you heart and soul." I will be there right beside you. I may not be out front, driving into war, but I'm the co-pilot, fighting with you for what is right and holy, right beside you.

As a Jonathan or an armor-bearer, be encouraged today to keep standing up and stepping out. Don't procrastinate and wait for the perfect conditions, but press on in Jesus' name.

If you know deep in your heart that you are a Saul and you really have no desire to change, there is absolutely no point in reading past this chapter. The rest of this book is about finding your purpose and passion in and through Christ to impact the world for His glory and your own adventure. That can't happen with the spirit of Saul ruling you. BUT—you have two possible moves, if you want to change.

First, if you do not know Christ as your Savior and Lord, go back to Chapter One and read through the Gospel presentation. There is no room in a heart filled with Christ for the spirit of Saul. If you invite Jesus in, Saul must leave. It is always going to take a while to mature and grow, so deep-seated sins and habits can sometimes take a while to drive out. But if your attitude changes to that of Christ, your actions and motives will soon follow. Obedience will bring healing and new life.

Lastly, if you know you're a Saul and you know for certain you have trusted Christ, then you may need to renew and re-establish your broken relationship with Him. Maybe unconfessed sin or apathy has crept in and caused great guilt and shame. If you bring that to Jesus today and hand it over to Him, He can cleanse and forgive. Check these out...

> *But if we confess our sins to God, he can always be trusted to forgive us and take our sins away. (1 John 1:9, CEV)*

> *So now there is no condemnation for those who belong to Christ Jesus. (Romans 8:1, NLT)*

> *The way to please you is to feel sorrow deep in our hearts. This is the kind of sacrifice you won't refuse. (Psalm 51:17, CEV)*

God didn't send His Son to die on a cross, defeat sin and death, and rise again, so that we could wallow around and beat ourselves up about our sin. He wants us to get up, ask forgiveness, move out, and mix faith with action in His name!

So, today, to know your passion and your purpose in this world, choose your role. Are you Jonathan or the Armor-bearer? He can use either to bring life and light to a lost and dying world.

CHAPTER 2 DISCUSSION QUESTIONS

1. What did you think of Jonathan and his armor bearer's method of attack?

2. Referring to the featured questions on Page 22—Are you waiting on anyone to take care of something for you? Is there a place where you are sitting on the sidelines? Share.

3. Are you an "armor bearer" to anyone? Is anyone an "armor bearer" to you? Discuss.

4. Is there any area of your life where you are being a "Saul?" Sitting back and waiting on someone else to take action? Discuss.

5. Talk about the mix of faith and action in a Christian's life. How do we balance them? What gets us out of balance?

6. Why do you think so many Christians today seem to be content with being "Saul?" What causes this?

7. How would/could the "spirit of Saul" keep you from finding your purpose and passion in Christ?

8. Discuss how you think a "Saul" can become a "Jonathan."

9. In most situations right now in your life, over-all, are you a "Saul," a "Jonathan," or an "armor bearer?" (Leader: Be sensitive, should any group members get honest in discussing this question, to offer grace and help to anyone that is struggling.)

10. Discuss the final paragraph—"God didn't send His Son to die on a cross, defeat sin and death, and rise again, so that we could wallow around and beat ourselves up about our sin. He wants us to get up, ask forgiveness, move out, and mix faith with action in His name!"

> **POST/TWEET**
>
> In the battle against evil, faith and action mixed together can rock the world through Christ. #stopwatchingstartdoing

CHAPTER 3

SO, WHAT IS YOUR GIFT?

There's a disturbing Scripture passage found in Luke where Jesus is teaching. It's interesting that this is a very often unused and untapped passage. You're about to see why, but it fits perfectly with this chapter.

> "Suppose one of you has a servant who comes in from plowing the field or tending the sheep. Would you take his coat, set the table, and say, 'Sit down and eat'? Wouldn't you be more likely to say, 'Prepare dinner; change your clothes and wait table for me until I've finished my coffee; then go to the kitchen and have your supper'? Does the servant get special thanks for doing what's expected of him? It's the same with you. When you've done everything expected of you, be matter-of-fact and say, 'The work is done. What we were told to do, we did.'" (Luke 17:7–10, MSG)

We listed the passage here from *The Message* Bible, but it has the same unnerving delivery, no matter what translation or paraphrase you read it in. As 21st century Christians, we tend to not like those dogmatic, we-aren't-in-control verses. We tend to like the ones that are more about us, such as "give you the desires of your heart," "more than you can ask or imagine," or "the abundant life."

So, why would we start off a chapter on spiritual gifts with a Scripture passage about duty and service? Simple, really. Although God does give you the option of free will to *not* recognize and use your gift; it is certainly your duty and service as a Christian to discover and exercise all the gifts and passions that God has uniquely placed in you. Why? Because when you do, that is when . . .

1—God is most glorified.

2—You are most satisfied.

3—The world will be most notified.

To break these 3 points down . . .

When you operate fully in your gifts and passion, this brings glory to your Creator. You are a reflection of His handiwork.

When you operate fully in your gifts and passion, you will be satisfied in your mind, body, and spirit. You will find your greatest and strongest contentment in living life for Him.

When you operate fully in your gifts and passion, the people around you, that you come in contact with, will see the difference in your life. "Notified" means to make something known or to tell officially. When your gifts are exercised and your passion for life is released, it is going to show!

> *You are like light for the whole world. A city built on top of a hill cannot be hidden, and no one would light a lamp and put it under a clay pot. A lamp is placed on a lampstand, where it can give light to everyone in the house. Make your light shine, so that others will see the good that you do and will praise your Father in heaven. (Matthew 5:14–16, CEV)*

Know this—God has most certainly placed both His gifts and passion inside of you that comes directly from His own heart. It is now up to you to find these, tap into them, and, through obedience, surrender them to His Spirit. We "do the work we were told to do." We "make our light shine."

WHATEVER THE QUESTION, THE ANSWER IS . . .

A worship leader at a large church sat down at the grand piano on the stage and began to play a beautiful melody, singing these words, "Yes, Lord. Yes, Lord." Soon the choir joined him in the new song. As the emotion swept over the congregation, people began standing to sing with the leader and choir, "Yes, Lord. Yes, Lord." Before long, the entire church was shaking the rafters with this simple repeated phrase, "Yes, Lord." The worship pastor quietly brought the music down low, and as he stopped, said, "Lord, you have heard our answer. Now what would you like us to do?"

I am sure at least some of those in attendance that day got caught up in the emotion and energy of the powerful song and then suddenly thought, "Whoa! Wait just a minute. I didn't mean I'd do *whatever* God wants! I was just singing a cool song and got caught up in the moment! Gimme a break!" ... But the worship leader had it exactly right!

As those saved by the shed blood of Christ from sin, eternal death, and Hell, we should rise up every morning saying, "God, my answer is yes to whatever You might ask me to do."

Before we can operate in our gift, we must be fully obedient, saying, "yes" to God. If we decide to filter out, pick and choose what we'll do and not do, then who is really our Lord?

THE CROSSROADS

For the rest of this chapter, we have to go down two different roads to explain this concept of gifts that God gives to each of us.

First, let's look at God's list of spiritual gifts.

> *So we are to use our different gifts in accordance with the grace that God has given us. If our gift is to speak God's message, we should do it according to the faith that we have; if it is to serve, we should serve; if it is to teach, we should teach; if it is to encourage others, we should do so. Whoever shares with others should do it generously; whoever has authority should work hard; whoever shows kindness to others should do it cheerfully. (Romans 12:6–8, GNT)*

God gives gifts to His followers for the purpose of building up His Body and reaching out to a lost world through us. We're going to take a look at the spiritual gifts given to each of us by the Holy Spirit and give you a short, working definition of each one. Although we have listed nine gifts and definitions, while the Romans passage only lists seven, the gifts we've listed are those typically drawn out of this passage by theologians. Explaining the unique differences between teaching, proclamation, pastoring, and evangelism is important in showing that all are needed aspects of leadership in the church.

Some translations also use the word "leadership" or "authority." While we don't list that specifically as a gift here, it is typically a strong quality found inside many of these gifts. Taking ownership or authority will often be a supernatural by-product of someone expressing his/her spiritual gifts.

Before you dig into these gifts, remember this: God gives the gifts and He chooses which ones He gives you, factoring in the personality and demeanor He made you with. He also chooses how and when you use them—IF you are following Him and listening to Him. Keep in mind, too, that God intended that these are all to be used with other believers working together. Others have gifts you don't have, but we all work together and share our gifts to build up the Body of Christ. This is about a team effort, not solo performances.

THE SPIRITUAL GIFTS

Evangelism—Telling people about Jesus.

You have a burning desire to make sure non-Christians hear about Christ. This person loves to talk about what Jesus can do for someone and how He can change a life. You desperately want to see Christ change lives. In short, talking about Jesus is very easy and natural. Communicating the Gospel is a deep, burning desire.

Proclamation/Preaching—Proclaiming God's Gospel message to the world.

This is sometimes called prophesy, but that word can also be associated with the telling of or prediction of the future, which is not our context here. Someone with the gift of proclamation will be bold and confident about speaking to a crowd about Christ and telling them how to be saved. They will speak the truth, no matter what it cost, in order to get God's message across.

Someone could be strong in evangelism, but not necessarily in proclamation or preaching. Someone with the gift of evangelism might love to share Christ one-on-one or in small groups, but not be good at speaking to a large group of people. While someone with the gift of proclamation may not be as good at one-on-one, he/she could speak to hundreds of people about how to be saved with no problem.

Pastor/Shepherding—Caring for the spiritual growth and needs of others.

There needs to be a shepherd for the sheep. A pastor will be a leader in God's Kingdom that people naturally trust and want to follow. This doesn't mean that the person with this gift has to be or will become a pastor. It simply means this person will actively care for people and their spiritual growth. They will often be attentive and concerned about specific problems or concerns people have, as well as discussing spiritual issues and being active in discipleship.

Like the evangelism/preaching comparison, a pastor/shepherd will, oftentimes, have the gift of teaching, but someone with the gift of teaching won't always have the gift of pastor/shepherding. For instance, a Bible study teacher or Christian college professor isn't always gifted at pastoring.

In today's large or "mega" churches, the person doing the teaching or preaching on Sunday morning often never pastors or shepherds people. In these churches, the person called the pastor actually is only a teacher, preacher, or evangelist, while others on the church staff operate in their gift of pastoring people.

Teaching—Explaining God's Word in a way that people can understand and apply.

Preaching is often about evangelism—winning people to Christ through the message—while teaching is often about discipleship—growing believers into mature Christians through the ministry of God's Word.

An evangelist or preacher will likely go from place to place speaking the same message of the Gospel—like Billy Graham did in his many crusades—but a teacher will often plant in one spot and raise up a group of believers.

Serving—Taking care of the details, often behind-the-scenes kind of work.

Whether it's a church service or a ministry project, someone has to do the "grunt work." Someone with the gift of service will enjoy the background toil and not get upset if they aren't recognized or praised. They enjoy being a part of the team, but not being the one in the spotlight. Any organization, but especially the church, needs a lot of people with this gift to make ministry function and flow well.

Encouragement/Exhortation—Communicating how God loves people and pointing out the good things He has given and done in someone.

Encouragers enjoy watching people succeed and helping them to do it. In our increasingly negative and critical culture, this is a much-needed ministry. We all know the value of someone that encourages us in our walk with Christ.

Giving/Contributing—Sharing money, resources, time, or energy to love and bless others.

Someone with the gift of giving won't necessarily have a lot of money, but be willing to give what they have. Those with this gift often are very good at motivating and inspiring others to give. In our ever-increasingly selfish culture, this is a vital gift to lead out in giving. We are all to give of our time and money to the church, but there are those that have an especially strong desire to give and want to lead out in seeing needs met.

Administration—Keeping everyone in line and moving in the right direction.

Administrators like details and making sure they get done. This is the business side of ministry, but a necessary part of the Kingdom life, keeping everything and everyone running smoothly and operating in excellence.

Mercy/Kindness—Caring for the helpless and the hurting.

This is a major part of the mission of the church. The sick, the poor, and the elderly are good examples of people that someone with the gift of mercy would want to help. This person will also be good at expressing and understanding God's grace. Someone with the gift of mercy feels others' pain and cares deeply about their welfare. A mercy person typically has a heart for the "underdog."

As a Christian, on a scale of 1 to 10, you will likely have some level of all of these gifts, even if it's a 1, simply because you have the desire. There will be several of them that will show to be your stronger gifts, say, between 5 and 8. But there will be one—maybe two—that will be a clear winner. You will find that when you practice your gift or strongest gifts, you can sense God's presence in a powerful way and you will see Him work in and through you, like you don't see when you use the other gifts.

SPIRITUAL GIFT EXERCISE #1

This exercise can help you "flesh out" or visualize these gifts. Look back through the list and think of someone that best matches each definition or description. Think about the people who *most* impact your life. For example, for pastor/shepherd, your best example may not be your church's pastor, but your small group leader, Sunday school teacher, or even a friend or relative. Write the name of the best example of the person who most displays this gift next to that paragraph in the margin of your book. This exercise will help you put flesh on a concept, to give a name of someone that you know both exhibits and exercises this gift. This can also help you see if you relate to someone with this gift.

SPIRITUAL GIFT EXERCISE #2

When you read through the gift list, which spiritual gift jumps out at you, or when you read the description, you think about your own life? If it helps, rule out the ones you know for sure *don't* describe you. But let us encourage you now to not be critical or negative about yourself. Clear all of that emotional noise away and be realistic about which of these gifts describe you and what you enjoy. Focus on your strengths. Which one sounds like you?

SPIRITUAL GIFT EXERCISE #3

Go to a more mature Christian that you deeply respect his/her own relationship with God. It would be great if you could think of two or three people. Go to them with the list of spiritual gifts, ask the person to scan it over, and then to tell you which gift or gifts they see in you. Ask them to explain why they feel that way and to give you any examples of ways they may have seen you display that gift or gifts. This is where God can use mature believers to confirm and affirm your gifts.

SPIRITUAL GIFT EXERCISE #4

If you should have a strong, mature group of Christian peers, such as a small group, ask them to look at the list and tell you what they see in you. This actually might be a great group exercise. Like Exercise #3, God can use the Body of Christ, through your peers, to confirm and affirm your gifts too.

There are some very good Spiritual Gift tests available. Many of them are structured so that you answer multiple choice or scaled questions and then, based on your answers, help you identify your gifts. You can check on-line, go to a Christian bookstore, or talk to a pastor at your church.

There is also a list of spiritual gifts in 1 Corinthians 12. We have chosen to focus our list on the Romans passage for the purpose of this book, because the Corinthians list begins to delve into areas that get into theological and denominational differences. To reach the majority of believers with this teaching, we want to avoid division by just having you understand that you have a spiritual gift and attempt to help you identify it. If your particular church, and/or family, focuses on gifts listed in Corinthians, that's great. Your church or family can help you with that list.

So, after doing some of the exercises and praying/searching the Romans 12 passage, write in what you believe your spiritual gift to be. If you're not certain, list your top three. But it's great if you now know, and are certain of, your one primary gift.

_____

_____

_____

TALENT GIFTS

Aside from the spiritual gifts God gives us, there are deeply personal and unique gifts that God has placed inside every person. These may be used in very public ways, but regardless, they will be used to bless people. Ironically, unlike the actual Biblical spiritual gifts listed in Romans 12 and 1 Corinthians 12, these gifts may be used completely outside of the Kingdom of God, even for personal glory. For the sake of definition, we're going to call these the "Talent Gifts." Gifts such as:

—An amazing singing voice

—An ability to play an instrument

—An incredible athletic ability

—A brilliant mind for science or math

—A unique ability to draw, sketch, paint, or create

—Uncanny ability to communicate—verbal or written

—A charisma to lead and motivate people

—Ability to articulate and explain difficult concepts simply

—Clean and organize messiness to look amazing

—Take something mechanical that's broken and fix it

—Work with wood or metal and create function or art

These are just a few examples to help you understand, but there are literally thousands more. All of us can think of athletes or some kind of celebrity that have used their talents as a platform to speak out about their faith in God.

In the 1981 Academy Award winning film, *Chariots of Fire*, the true story of Eric Lidell, the Scotsman who ran in the 1924 Olympics, there is a scene where his sister is deeply concerned, because she feels his running is pulling him away from their commitment to

SO, WHAT IS YOUR GIFT?

go to China together as missionaries. He looks deep into his sister's eyes and says, "I believe God made me for a purpose, but he also made me fast. And when I run, I feel His pleasure." Eric ran in the Olympics, but also did go on to serve the Lord in China.

One of the most beautiful, yet amazing ways that we know we are using our gift and tapping into the heart of God is when we can "feel His pleasure" as Eric explained to his sister. It's that feeling deep down that this activity you are engaged in is a gift from your Creator and why you are on this planet. It's a part of you that just feels natural and right to do. Or maybe better said—*super*natural and right to do.

We have all seen the beaming face of a dad whose child just took their first steps, rode their bike without training wheels, brought home their best test grade ever, kicked their first soccer goal, or graduated from school. We know that look. That pride. That pleasure. That is magnified a zillion times with God, the Father. God—your Father. He shows that deep pride from His heart to ours when we take what He has uniquely placed into us and display it to the world.

So, what is "that thing" that you feel like you would die if you could no longer do? "That thing" that you love to do, can't wait to do, can't live without? "That thing" that you just feel is why God put you on the Earth? And "that thing" that you know your Father enjoys seeing and hearing you do?

Write down in the space provided below what you believe your Talent Gift is. If you aren't certain, write down what you love to do. Maybe you can think of several things. Write them down in this space.

.

_____

_____

_____

There are two very strong, distinct differences in the spiritual gifts that God gives and the talent gifts that God gives.

The talent gifts are given to you upon your creation. When God made you, He put that in your soul.

The spiritual gifts are given to you only after your salvation and surrender to Him. He places that in you upon your redemption.

The talent gifts can be used whether you ever become a Christian or not, and can be used for your own glory, and not God's. Obviously though, His intention when He gave you the gift was for you to give it back to Him for His glory.

The spiritual gifts will be used only under the leadership and direction of the Holy Spirit and for God's glory. Without Him, they don't work.

That is why you can see so many athletes and artists use amazing talent all for their own glory and gain. God gave the gift, made them a steward, but He also allowed them the choice as to what they do with it and who it glorifies.

There are countless times that artists and athletes, who very publicly live immoral and irresponsible lives, stand and thank God after winning an award. This is always a sobering realization that so many people know they have a gift from God, but have no idea how to give it back for His glory.

> Is there a talent you know God has given you to use for Him, but so far you have used it for yourself? If so, don't beat yourself up about it. Continue reading, give it to Him, and He'll help you figure out what to do next.

USING YOUR GIFTS WISELY

Let's switch back to the spiritual gifts now. When we operate inside and within our spiritual gifts, God always demonstrates His purpose through us, in the gifts. There is evidence of the Holy Spirit working in and through us—individually and as a body of believers. Here are some instructional verses from 1 Corinthians about gifts.

A spiritual gift is given to each of us so we can help each other. (1 Corinthians 12:7, NLT)

"All these are the work of one and the same Spirit, and he gives them to each one, just as he determines." (1 Corinthians 12:11, NIV)

God gives each Christian a gift from Him for the purpose of serving and helping the other believers.

When we do not operate in our gifts, or begin to take on too much and overlap into other's gifts, then ...

1. We can stifle—hinder or stop—the Holy Spirit. He is unable to use us, because we are not giving our life to His service.

2. We can stifle someone else's gifts. When we do something in the Kingdom that God never intends for us to do, we rob someone else of the joy and opportunity to use their gift.

"But God has combined the members of the body and has given greater honor to the parts that lacked it, so that there should be no division in the body, but that its parts should have equal concern for each other. If one part suffers, every part suffers with it; if one part is honored, every part rejoices with it." (1 Corinthians 12:24b-2,6 NIV)

As we learn to use our gifts, God brings:

—**Invitations**

He wants you to experience being involved with Him in the work of His Kingdom. He will invite you to that work regularly, offering you clear opportunities to use your gifts.

—**Limitations**

We are to discover what our gifts are *and* what they are *not*. When we live within our gifts, we have to defer to others who have what we don't have or are stronger in that area than us.

Two things will result from understanding your limitations:
1. Interdependence on Biblical community—relying on other believers
2. Personal humility—not relying on yourself

Paul had learned the beauty of realizing his interdependence on others and how God uses His servants.

In 1 Corinthians 3:5-6 (MSG), he states, *"Who do you think Paul is, anyway? Or Apollos, for that matter? Servants, both of us—servants who waited on you as you gradually learned to entrust your lives to our mutual Master. We each carried out our servant assignment. I planted the seed, Apollos watered the plants, but God made you grow. It's not the one who plants or the one who waters who is at the center of this process but God, who makes things grow."*

Our gifting and limits are God's sovereign determination to maximize our impact on the world. A gift is a huge responsibility, but God has allowed for individuals to fit into their part of that task when used correctly.

> *"May they be brought to complete unity to let the world know that you sent me and have loved them even as you have loved me. Father, I want those you have given me to be with me where I am, and to see my glory, the glory you have given me because you loved me before the creation of the world. Righteous Father, though the world does not know you, I know you, and they know that you have sent me. I have made you known to them, and will continue to make you known in order that the love you have for me may be in them and that I myself may be in them." (Jesus' prayer in John 17:23b-26, NIV)*

In closing, take a look at the 3D version of what your gifts from God are for and what your responsibility is.

DISCOVER   **DEFINE**   **DEVELOP**

1. Discover your passion.
   Know what fires you up and glorifies God!
2. Define your calling.
   How does God want you to use your gift in the world?
3. Develop your ministry.
   When your gift and obedience meets God's power and presence, look out!

As we press on, you'll begin to see life in 3D as you discover, define, and develop your gift and ministry.

The goal of this chapter was to help you realize how God has uniquely outfitted you with a gift or gifts from Him, to be used by you through His power to reach the world.

Are the two blank spaces in this chapter filled in yet? If not, be sure and complete the four exercises in this chapter to find out. Before you move forward in this book, it would be best for you to know your gifts. If you know now, let's go!

CHAPTER 3 DISCUSSION QUESTIONS

1. What are your thoughts about the Luke 17:7–10 passage? What do you think Jesus' point was? What was He communicating to us?

2. Why do you think God would give us spiritual gifts and then place the responsibility on us to discover and use them?

3. How do you think our personal obedience factors into God's ability to use us—and our gifts? Why would obedience matter?

4. Was there any of the spiritual gifts listed that you didn't understand how they are to be used? Discuss.

5. Have you done any of the Exercises listed to find your gifts? Which exercises did you do? What did you find out?

6. Why are the Talent Gifts often easier to see and understand? Did this explanation help you connect your Talent Gift to your faith?

7. Did the Eric Lidell example make sense to you? Can you fill in the blank now: "When I _____ , I feel God's pleasure." Would anyone like to share his/her sentence?

8. Why do you think God would give us gifts, but then give us free will to use them for Him or not?

9. Now that you hopefully know your spiritual gift and how your talent gift from God can be used, do you think it will be easier for you to spot when He is sending you invitations to use them for Him?

10. How might God use your gifts and passion in a ministry to people? Share.

> **POST/TWEET**
> Discover your passion. Define your calling. Develop your ministry. #stopwatchingstartdoing

CHAPTER 4

SO, WHAT'S STOPPING YOU?

Once you determine your spiritual gift and talent gift (or gifts), coupled with God-given passion, an important next step is to look at the roadblocks on your journey. You may not be able to do anything about some of these, while others are fully removable and need to be dealt with. Roadblocks need to be determined, sized up, and then a plan put in place to remove any obstacles that could possibly hinder your spiritual growth and progress.

In this chapter, we will walk through many of the common hindrances to exercising your gifts and what can be done about them. We'll start with you and then zoom out to your circles of influence, but first, let's take a look at someone from the Bible that struggled with receiving his gift from God. As you read about Moses, think about your own life and relate his story to yourself. He pressed on to become a great man of God and a leader of God's people, just as you can.

SELF-DOUBT

> *But Moses protested again, "What if they won't believe me or listen to me? What if they say, 'The Lord never appeared to you'?" (Exodus 4:1, NLT)*

Self-doubt is a huge roadblock to receiving God's gift. Very often, it's not that we question God, but ourselves. We believe He can, but that we can't! But who is that focus on—God or us?

The key to stopping self-doubt is not so much to believe in yourself, but to put your eyes on Christ. Self-confidence is not a sin, pride is. But often the jump from self-doubt to self-confidence is very tough, so daily surrendering our hearts to Christ and placing our trust in Him will start to shift our lives to being God-centered, not self-focused. And lead us away from self-doubt.

God asked a very odd question in response to Moses' questions. In fact, God essentially ignored the protest.

> *Then the Lord asked him, "What is that in your hand?"* (Exodus 4:2a, NLT)

We spent all of chapter 3 giving you the tools to discover your gift and passion. The point was for you to see "what is in your hand," as God was trying to help Moses see.

Stopping self-doubt in its tracks is only done through complete and total surrender to Jesus Christ. Focus on God. Eyes on Him.

Let's move on to our next roadblock and Moses' answer to God's question.

FEAR

> *"A shepherd's staff," Moses replied. "Throw it down on the ground," the Lord told him. So Moses threw down the staff, and it turned into a snake! Moses jumped back.* (Exodus 4:2b–3, NLT)

Fear can be a giant roadblock to what God is doing. Many people would rather suffer in mediocrity and anonymity than face their fear of what God might have them do.

We also know fear is one of the enemy's most effective tactics. When we fear, we are not expressing faith. Faith diminishes fear. They are opposites. It's like an empty glass. The only way to get the air out is to pour liquid in. When we are afraid, the only real solution is to pour faith into our souls, thereby pushing fear out.

Author and teacher Dr. Neil Anderson says, "Fear can cause us to hang onto the trunk, while the fruit is found out on the limb."

Moses was obedient. Even though it probably sounded very strange to him, he threw his staff down. And there is no way he could have predicted what God would do next! "Snake! What?!"

Only one weapon can effectively fight the obstacle of fear and that is faith. Express visible, active faith in Christ.

THE TURNING POINT

> *Then the Lord told him, "Reach out and grab its tail." So Moses reached out and grabbed it, and it turned back into a shepherd's staff in his hand.* (Exodus 4:4, NLT)

Here the tide turns. God is winning Moses over. Moses begins to forget about his doubt and fear to express his faith.

Author and communicator Henry Blackaby coined the phrase years ago in his *Experiencing God* resources: a "crisis of belief." A crisis of belief is the turning point where a Christian has to decide to express faith and believe God versus doubting and fearing. It's a put-up-or-shut-up moment of "are you going to believe or not?"

Moses stood at his turning point and trusted God. He reached down and picked up a snake, just because God told him to. This single moment would be the beginning of literally thousands of faith exchanges between God and Moses.

There is another very important point we cannot miss here — Moses was giving his staff to God and God was giving it back to him, but everything had now changed. Yet in the end, the staff didn't change—Moses did! The Moses that picked up the staff was a different Moses than the man who had thrown the staff down. Those few moments were life-changing for this man.

Our main goal with this book is to guide you to these turning points between yourself and God, just as Moses did—moments in time that change eternity.

SO, WHAT'S STOPPING YOU?

OUR HANDS + GOD'S PLANS

"Perform this sign," the Lord told him. "Then they will believe that the Lord, the God of their ancestors—the God of Abraham, the God of Isaac, and the God of Jacob—really has appeared to you." (Exodus 4:5, NLT)

Here's what happened for Moses. God wanted his hands, not his plans. He wanted Moses to offer himself for His service. God calls each of us to this same destination—to give Him our hands and give up our plans. We must die to our own agenda.

Here's a couple of examples...

A talented football player always prays before games that God would bless him and protect him—and, of course, help him to win. A submitted Christ follower who also plays football commits his talent and platform to Christ, asking God to use him however he sees fit to witness to his teammates and coaches to reach people.

An up and coming young female singer prays before shows with her band, goes to church when she can, and thanks God anytime she wins anything or gets praised. A submitted Christ follower, who is also a singer, knows that any fame or opportunity she has is because God is growing her boundaries for her to be a light and a witness for Him. She knows she is a role model and takes her behavior very seriously as a reflection on Christ.

Do you see the differences here? We've all seen the people who use God as some sort of good luck charm versus the believers who are really shining His Light out there. Author Kyle Idleman calls it the difference in being a fan or a follower. A fan is on board for the popularity ride, while a follower is there no matter what.

We can't say, "God, bless my plans while I use my hands as I wish." We have to confess, "God, I realize what You have placed in my hands. Now take it and bless Your plans."

So, here's the question... Have you truly committed your hands to God and let go of your plans? Have you given God your gifts and talents? Have you come to Him and declared, "I will use my gifts for WHATEVER You bring to me?"

The story is told that in one of President Abraham Lincoln's cabinet meetings, he shared with those gathered that he needed their full trust on an issue. Due to the national security issues and confidentiality at play, he had to ask each one to sign off on their support without knowing the full details of the document. Each man, out of his deep trust, respect, and honor for Lincoln, signed the document. We don't know the end result of this situation, but we do see what a man of character can produce in his followers.

This is exactly what God asks of each of us—to sign off on a declaration that we will do whatever He asks of us—without full knowledge of the details. Trust and honor in exchange for His deep love and commitment for us.

So many people come to God and say, "Okay, here's what I'm willing to do, but, first, . . ." However, God is not interested in making deals and negotiation. He's looking for those who are ready and willing to join Him in changing the world.

The Lord searches all the earth for people who have given themselves completely to him. He wants to make them strong. (2 Chronicles 16:9a, NCV)

Let's move on with Moses.

Then the Lord said to Moses, "Now put your hand inside your cloak." So Moses put his hand inside his cloak, and when he took it out again, his hand was white as snow with a severe skin disease. "Now put your hand back into your cloak," the Lord said. So Moses put his hand back in, and when he took it out again, it was as healthy as the rest of his body. (Exodus 4:6–7, NLT)

God wanted Moses to see the change He can bring. God performed a miracle on Moses to show Him the incredible power He had to do anything, anytime, to anyone.

God will take your gift and change it into an amazing connection to people and, in the process, change you as well through His activity. Just as God showed Moses how He could change his hand leprous and back, diseased to healthy, He can change you and others in and through your gift, given and submitted to Him.

Here's a personal testimony from Robert (one of the authors): "Since I was about 6 years old, I was frequently told by people that I had a 'God-given gift' of drumming. I didn't mind people saying that, because I knew it was a very natural thing for me to play drums and I saw it move people. But I didn't know this God Who people said had given me this gift!

"That changed, at 19 years old, when I was introduced to Jesus through some friends who cared enough to tell me. So, having played rock music for several years, I packed up my drums, put them away in storage, and actually thought I was done. Playing rock music with who I played it with, where I played it, and what all went on there, I didn't figure I should do it anymore, if I was going to walk with God. I gave up the gift, thinking I couldn't use it for Him.

"Just a few months later, a music minister at a church played some songs for me from some Christian artists and within a few months, I was not only playing drums again, but playing music that glorified and led people to Him. But in that three short months, God made an amazing transition in me where I understood my gift was now His. It was indeed God-given, as so many people had told me, but now I had given it back! And then, for the next 10 years, I played all over the country, before hundreds of thousands of people, sharing God's message of salvation through music. My hands and His plans."

THE ASSIGNMENT

So Moses went back home to Jethro, his father-in-law. "Please let me return to my relatives in Egypt," Moses said. "I don't even know if they are still alive." "Go in peace," Jethro replied. Before Moses left Midian, the Lord said to him, "Return to Egypt, for all those who wanted to kill you have died." So Moses took his wife and sons, put them on a donkey, and headed back to the land of Egypt. In his hand he carried the staff of God. —Exodus 4:18-20 NLT

Notice the Scripture says that Moses was carrying the staff of God, not his staff. Everything had changed. God had intervened. Moses had accepted his destiny led by God. God had effectively removed Moses' personal roadblocks, namely self-doubt and fear. He had brought Moses to a turning point and through a crisis of belief. And now Moses believed—that God can and will. And does.

So, have you put your own story up against Moses? Where are you with your self-doubt and fear? Are you at a turning point? In a crisis of belief with your gift or have you accepted and submitted it to God? Have you signed off on giving it to Him, no matter what He asks? Have you surrendered your hands to His plans?

> **Addictions are a stark reality today in many lives. If you struggle with a constant temptation and sin, there is no better time than right now to deal with and ask for help. Talk to a pastor, counselor, or a Christian friend that you can trust and hand this over now for the right help and full surrender to God.**

Before we move on to other obstacles and roadblocks outside of ourselves, please be sure that you have taken a serious look at your own heart and dealt with anything that you know is standing in the way. God wants to and is ready to help you deal with anything, just as He did with Moses.

YOUR FAMILY

The first thing we have to establish is that God wants to use you in your family before any other place of ministry. It will typically be the toughest place to minister, but it's the first priority on the list to God. For a Christian wanting to follow the Lord and be effective, there are two types of families—supportive and non-supportive. Let's start with supportive.

The positives are obvious. You want to walk with God daily and exercise your gifts from Him and they want you to as well. But here are some things to watch out for . . .

YOU need to discover your spiritual gifts and talents. While a spouse, parent, or other Christian family member should definitely be a major part of your counsel and confirmation, you must determine what your gifts are. When anyone tells you what God is saying or has for you and you just go with it without consulting Him, then that person (or persons) becomes your "priest"—meaning a mediator between you and God. You need to seek God on your own and allow Him to speak to you regarding your gifts. To be clear—crucial family members should speak into your life, encourage you toward the discovery of your gifts, and also help affirm your gifts. The only thing we are cautioning against here is you being told that you have a certain gift, you just accepting it, and attempting to function in it without consulting God or praying through the search for yourself.

If your family and church are supportive of your relationship with God, you should be very grateful for an amazing support system.

Now, if you are in a family that is not supportive, likely because they are not Christians, there is bad news and good news for you.

The bad news is obvious. You may be misunderstood, persecuted, and possibly even ridiculed. Family members can think someone has become a part of a cult or is "brainwashed." The good news is that dealing with this in a manner that reflects Christ can strengthen your faith in incredible ways. Maintaining your witness in a non-Christian family can grow and mature you in a way like nothing else can.

Some families are neutral and won't encourage or discourage you. Your faith is just your choice and they will simply tolerate it. Other families may have a wrong concept of what Christianity really is. Maybe a family member had a bad experience with a church or minister in the past, or some other event, that caused a barrier towards God.

A very important point to remember, regarding any non-Christian family members, is that it is extremely difficult to find anyone who has been debated or argued into the Kingdom of God. Most people make a decision to follow Christ through understanding His truth, love, and grace, not through someone presenting a stronger argument or overwhelming them with spiritual facts. Steady, faithful obedience, and grace can win over anyone, especially family members, more than any other approach. Remember—consistency, not condemnation.

Here's another personal testimony from Robert: "When I turned my life over to Christ at age 19, I also surrendered to the ministry. I had moved away from home, but still lived in the same town as my parents. My father continually questioned my newfound faith with comments like, "The way you're thinking now isn't reality. You'll wake up one day to the real world and see that," and "You don't really know what you're doing. You're too young to make a decision like this." My dad was speaking out of a disillusioned frame of mind from his own past. Unfortunately, just a few months later, my father died. But I was able to talk with my mom and lead her to Christ at age 48. As hard as that family experience was, it strengthened my own faith in incredible ways."

If you happen to be a young person that is still at home, many teens that live in non-Christian homes ask where to draw the line in honoring and obeying parents and honoring God. As much as it is possible, obey your parents. If they ask you to do something that you believe is ungodly, immoral, or against Biblical instruction, first, explain that you are uncomfortable with their request and then ask them to please excuse you from what they are asking. If needed, explain that it is against your spiritual beliefs, but be careful to not sound "holier than thou" or superior. Most of the time a loving parent will understand and agree. If anything occurs that you are in question about or concerned for, talk to your pastor as soon as possible.

If you are an adult in a marriage with a non-Christian, these same principles of grace and honor apply to your marriage as well.

Regardless of the spiritual foundation of your family, it is no coincidence that you are where you are, in the family you are in. God has strategically placed you there. Serve and honor Him by serving and honoring your family—Christian or non-Christian.

Serve wholeheartedly, as if you were serving the Lord, not people, because you know that the Lord will reward each one for whatever good they do . . . (Ephesians 6:7–8a, NIV)

YOUR FRIENDS

Friends can fall into the same category as family, except friends can often make or break someone's walk with God. Where many people either don't care or feel neutral about what their family thinks, they may care a great deal about friends' opinions. Far too many Christians have not only pushed their gifts and passions aside because of friends, but literally left the faith because of their influence.

Don't fool yourselves. Bad friends will destroy you. (1 Corinthians 15:33, CEV)

So what do you do when friends reject you because of your faith, sometimes even Christian friends? Well, first, you have now seen their true colors and know that certain things are more important than your friendship. But, just as Jesus did, you must continue to show love toward them, pray for them, and express your friendship, regardless of their response. This will be the best representation of Christ you could make.

There are many times, however, that friends will respond very positively about your faith, even want to know more about your decision, and what you believe.

For most people, friends will either be an amazing distraction from faith or an incredible support system for it. It rarely remains neutral. There are those times when someone has decided to follow Christ and has to separate from friends in order to grow and mature. It's not about hating on anyone; it's a matter of making the choice to walk with God and go His way, no longer being led by "the crowd."

In a very real way when Jesus was choosing His closest disciples, He was also choosing those who would be His closest friends. These men and women were far from perfect, but learned from Jesus—and each other—to go on and change the world. Take Peter, for example, a man who went from denying Jesus to leading the early church. His friendship with Christ changed His life. As a result, those who befriended Peter had their lives changed as well. That's the power of friendships and close relationships.

> *Then Jesus said to them all, "If anyone wants to follow Me, he must give up himself and his own desires. He must take up his cross everyday and follow Me. (Luke 9:23, NLV)*

> *Whoever is not with me is against me, and whoever does not gather with me scatters. (Matthew 12:30, NIV)*

So, to move forward in your faith and operate in your gifts, an evaluation of friends is essential. Here are some options to consider as you pray about your friends.

    1. You must have some Christian friends to encourage you in your faith, as you should them.

2. *Friends that tempt you or drag you down in your faith may have to become history. Unfortunately, this could include some Christian friends.*

3. *Some friends who are neutral faith-wise—you may be able to turn the tables and begin to lead them to Christ or lead back into a close relationship with Him.*

The goal for you as an active Christ-follower, exercising your spiritual gifts and moving in your God-given passion, should be to have healthy relationships all the way from your self-image to your family to friends, and out to all your circles of influence.

God's plan for you is to be an agent of change for Him. He desires to use you strategically in every area of life. Removing personal roadblocks and engaging in healthy relationships will set a strong pattern for you to be an effective witness for Christ your entire life.

CHAPTER 4 DISCUSSION QUESTIONS

1. Discuss how self-doubt can interfere with using your gifts and passion for Christ?

2. Why should the Christian work on developing a God-focus, rather than just a stronger self-confidence?

3. Talk about how fear can hinder, or even stop, you from using your gifts and passion.

4. What are some practical ways you can build your faith to the point of stopping fear?

5. Do you feel like you have faced a turning point yet with your gift and passion? If so, talk about that. If not, where are you in that process?

6. Why do you think God wants us to give Him our hands, but give up our plans?

7. Talk about your family and their position on your faith, gifts, and passion for God. (Keep it as positive as possible.)

8. Discuss your friends' impact on your faith. Encouraging? Discouraging? Neutral?

9. How do you think friends can impact the use of your gifts and passion?

10. Are there any roadblocks to your gift—that weren't covered in the chapter—that you struggle with? Discuss.

POST/TWEET

God can take your gift and change it into an amazing connection to people and, in the process, change you as well. #stopwatchingstartdoing

CHAPTER 5

WHAT NEED IN THE WORLD MATCHES YOUR GIFT?

A man who was attending seminary to become a pastor asked to talk to me one afternoon. I could quickly tell that he was very frustrated about something. As he sat down, I asked, "Okay, tell me what's up?" He blurted out, "I have a strong calling from God to reach the lost. I just want to reach lost people!" I responded, "Yeah, I know that about you. So what's the problem?" Again, he said with frustration, "That's it! I want to preach the Gospel and win people to Christ! Where do I start? Where do I begin?"

The young minister's problem was no longer "what." He knew what "what" was. He had identified and established his gift and passion. The "what" was now very clear to him. The new problem was now the "how." To use an analogy, evangelism, specifically through Biblical preaching, was his "gun," so to speak. But where does he shoot? What's the target?

To continue this analogy, often when we identify our gift and passion, it's like being handed a shotgun. The shells for many shotguns are loaded with scatter-shot, because it's hundreds of BBs, so that when the trigger is pulled, they go out—and everywhere. When we find our "how" for the "what," we trade in the shotgun for a sniper rifle with a scope—a specific target where your shots count.

It's the same issue that many university graduates have. They hold a degree in a specific area, but now need the job to do the work they are trained to do. It's like being a train engine with no track—lots of power with nowhere to go.

For your gift and passion, this is where God enters the picture in a big way.

Take our seminary student with the gift of evangelism through preaching. He finds out there are five large jails and a prison within a 200-mile radius of his home. He goes and meets with law enforcement and the chaplains involved at those facilities. He begins to hold services there on a regular basis where he preaches the Gospel. Men and women, desperate and searching for answers, hear the Good News and come to Christ. "What" meets "how."

A young lady feels that her gifts are service and administration, while her passion is the homeless. She begins to volunteer at a local shelter and food pantry where things are fairly disorganized. Within a few weeks, she has cleaned up, re-arranged, and organized the pantry and kitchen, making the ministry more efficient in its operation. Not only will she now volunteer weekly to serve, but she can also maintain the order that she put into place using her gifts to the fullest. "What" meets "how."

A young man identifies his gift of mercy and that his passion is helping children. A nearby city has a children's hospital, so he goes through the paperwork and background check to start visiting there once a week, reading a book or working a puzzle, or ministering to recovering children. "What" meets "how."

See? In each example, it's matching your gift with a need in the world that fuels your passion for life and God.

JUST ONE LIFE

Hunger

Clean Water

Human Trafficking

Poverty

Disease

Terminal Illness

Child Abuse

Orphans

Education

Homeless

AIDS

Sounds like the evening news, doesn't it?

These are just a few of the thousands of problems that need solving in the world. It is SO easy to look at this list and allow it to overwhelm us. So much so that many, many people just throw up their hands and say there's no way they can make a difference, so they don't. Ever.

This is where most people just start watching.

But this is where an omniscient and sovereign God can assign each of us to our role and we ALL make a difference where we are placed. So—we each must find our spot, our place to meet a need, and meet it. If you have a burden to help people, is it better to be overwhelmed and never help anyone or to help one person each month? Well, one is always better than none.

So, by now, after working through the first four chapters, you should know your gift or gifts, which is your "what." Now, we go after the "how."

We have just one life to live and give. We can't clone ourselves and go after several world issues. We have to decide and shoot at a target. We must choose where God has for us and go after that cause or place.

REFINING YOUR HOW

The following is a list of questions to help you begin to figure out the "how" to the "what." There is a blank line for you to write in any thoughts you have.

WHAT NEED IN THE WORLD MATCHES YOUR GIFT?

Is there a nation outside the United States that you have a burden or a unique interest in? If you feel called only to the U.S., write that down.

_____

If you wrote down a nation outside the U.S., is there a certain people group there that you have a burden or an interest in? (Ex. Australia—Aborigines)

_____

If you wrote down the U.S., is there a certain people group or race that you have a burden or an interest in? (Ex. Kenyan refugees living in New York City)

_____

If you wrote down the U.S., is there a certain region, state, or city that you have a burden or an interest in? (Ex. inner city Chicago)

_____

Is there a specific gender you feel called to minister to? (Ex. impoverished women in Africa.)

_____

Is there a particular age group that you have a burden for? (Ex. Orphans birth to 5 in India. Be as specific as you can.)

_____

Is there a particular economic segment of your chosen nation you feel called to? (Ex. millionaires in Dubai.)

_____

Is there an activity, sport, talent, knowledge, skill, or hobby that you want to connect to ministry with others? (Soccer with children in Mexico, teaching farming skills to Haitians)

Do you feel what you do will win people to Christ—evangelism?

Do you feel what you do will help Christians grow in Christ—discipleship?

Do you feel what you do will "plant seeds" for people to get closer to faith or closer to a relationship with Christ? (Some call this pre-evangelism.)

Write down the one area of these three that you feel best describes what you will do.

If you look at the answers you wrote down, it should begin to refine your "how." Here's some examples of answers:

France—Paris—university students—teach English—plant seeds

OR

U.S.—Appalachian area—children under 12—unemployed households—tutoring—evangelism

OR

Haiti—rural areas—families—farmers—agricultural help—discipleship through assistance of local pastor/church

Get the idea? Please DO NOT be influenced by the examples. They are only included to be certain you fully understand how the questions can help lead you to your own answer and to whom you can minister—your "how."

Prayerfully consider the information you have worked through so far. Remember, it is a smart move to get counsel from your pastor or a solid Christian friend as you work through this process. Receiving confirmation and affirmation from those that know and love you can be very helpful for you to discern how and where the Lord is leading you.

WHAT ABOUT GOING TO COLLEGE OR GRADUATE SCHOOL?

You may be heading to college soon or are in college or grad school now. Maybe you've been in the work force for quite a while and have been considering going back to school, because of your calling. If you've already discerned that God is leading you to school, or even to a particular higher learning institute, that's great. If that is the case, then "bloom where you're planted," as they say. Find a situation as close as you can get to what you sense God is telling you. You may need to use some of the specific information you have written down as a future goal and a prayer commitment for now.

For example, even if you have a burden for Iraqi children and can't go to Iraq now, find out if there are any Iraqi refugees anywhere in your area. Plus praying for your particular place of burden can be a powerful way to connect spiritually right now. So much of your ministry burden can be touched right where you are. There are children, elderly, poor, hungry, and illiterate all around you. Whatever your calling, you can find a place of ministry. Whether God has you somewhere for the next year or four years, don't wait until you have the perfect conditions to minister, because the chances are you'll never do it. You'll start watching! Do—right where you are. Then when you are free to move on, head toward His calling and place of ministry as specifically as you can!

YOU GOT THIS!

It is so easy for any of us to feel like we have nothing to give or that we might never be able to excel with the passion we've been given. That is simply not true.

One of the most amazing and inspirational stories of how one simple person can change the world is that of Mother Teresa. She died in 1997 at the age of 87, after over 45 years of sacrifice and service to the poorest of the poor in Calcutta and other ministry centers that she established around the world. She was born Agnes Gonxha Bojaxhiu in Macedonia to devout Catholic parents. Her father died when she was only nine. As early as twelve, Agnes felt a call to the life of Christian service. Although her mother was initially against the idea of her beloved daughter leaving home to become a nun, she eventually understood the call and gave Agnes this piece of prophetic advice, "Put your hand in His hand and walk all alone with Him." This charge would mark Mother Teresa's life for the rest of her days.

Her work eventually established the Order of Missionaries of Charity with work in over 130 countries worldwide including a network of over 600 homeless shelters, orphanages, AIDS hospices, leprosy clinics, and homes for single mothers.

A Gallup Poll survey in 2000, reflecting on the 20th Century, named her first on the list of "The Most Widely Admired People of the Century." This tiny woman with a huge vision from God was never wealthy or powerful by the world's standards, but no one can deny that her life changed the world forever.

Many of the people over the history of mankind that made major contributions to the Kingdom of God had two key ingredients that caused their success. The good news is that you can have these as well. They are . . .

1. Availability

    A wise man once said, "The world is changed by those who show up." That's being available.

2. Obedience

    Jesus stated in John 14:15, *"If you love me, you will obey what I command."*

Why was Mother Teresa able to become one of the most admired figures in the world, while taking care of the dying in the slums of Calcutta? She was available and obedient to God.

How was Moses able to lead a nation and perform miracles in the name of God? He was available and obedient to God.

How was Paul able to shepherd and sustain so many of the early churches? He was available and obedient to God.

> Regardless of your self-esteem, self-image, what anyone may have told you before, or what you believe about yourself, you must come to the conclusion today that all God requires is your availability and obedience to do great things with you. Simply decide if you will believe that truth.

How was Jesus able to redeem us in our sin and take the keys of death and Hell from Satan? He was available and obedient to God.

How will you take your passion for God, your gifts, and your calling to change the world? You'll be available and obedient to God.

Author and speaker Bob Goff says, "Everyone wants to make a difference in the world, but few will actually decide to be different than the world to do it."

It's really quite simple, yet extremely hard to follow through, because the world is literally going the other way. But, if you're ready, you got this! You can certainly do it through the power and direction of the Holy Spirit.

ONE BIG WORLD AND YOU

The world is huge. There are billions of people. There are thousands of massive problems and major tragedies daily. You're just one person. You have doubts. You fail. You aren't certain you can handle what God gives you ... Congratulations! You are quite human. Here's the great, great news. God is huge. He created all those people. He knows how to solve every problem that man has created. He created you with a specific personality, skill set, gifting, and spirit that are totally unique to you. No one else can do what you do, exactly the way you can do it. Nobody! There is work to do that He intends for only you to do. No one else. He wants to empower you, walk with you, and lead you to and through an incredible journey with Him.

So—what need does God want only you to meet, as only you can do, with only Him to help you? "Take His hand and walk all alone with Him." Be available. Be obedient. Stop watching! Start doing!

> *The person who trusts me will not only do what I'm doing but even greater things, because I, on my way to the Father, am giving you the same work to do that I've been doing. You can count on it. From now on, whatever you request along the lines of who I am and what I am doing, I'll do it. That's how the Father will be seen for who he is in the Son. I mean it. Whatever you request in this way, I'll do. (John 14:11b–13, MSG)*

CHAPTER 5 DISCUSSION QUESTIONS

1. Why do you think the "what" is often easier to figure out than the "how?"

2. Do you think a Christian can figure out his/her "what," but then just keep watching? Why or why not?

3. Why do you feel most of us get overwhelmed by the world's problems, to the point of paralyzing our actions?

4. Let's talk about what you found with the "Refining Your How" section. (Facilitator: There are intentionally less questions for this chapter, so you can spend plenty of time talking about this crucial part of the book.)

5. How can/does further education fit into expanding your passion and gift?

6. Discuss any roadblocks you may have for being available and obedient.

> **POST/TWEET**
>
> God uniquely created you! No one else can do what you do, exactly the way you can do it. #stopwatchingstartdoing

CHAPTER 6

CAN YOU STOP WATCHING?

Check out these three different people, found in Luke 9:57–62, who talked with Jesus about following Him.

Along the way someone said to Jesus, "I'll go anywhere with you!" Jesus said, "Foxes have dens, and birds have nests, but the Son of Man doesn't have a place to call his own. (CEV)

Translation:
Person: "Woo hoo! I'll go anywhere with You, Jesus! You rock!"
Jesus: "But, I don't have a home, we camp out a lot, and live off the land."
Person: "Oh ... okay ... maybe some other time!"

Jesus told someone else to come with him. But the man said, "Lord, let me wait until I bury my father." Jesus answered, "Let the dead take care of the dead, while you go and tell about God's kingdom." (CEV)

I know Jesus' response sounds really harsh and cold, but here's the deal. There is a strong likelihood, due to cultural norms of the day, that this man's father was old, but not yet dead. He was saying to Jesus, in essence, "I need to go take care of my family, but as soon as dad is gone, and I get the inheritance, I'll meet up with you." Jesus knew how long He had and that He didn't have time for people to delay their obedience. The Kingdom of God was at hand! Time was short and the opportunity was now—not later.

Here's a major principle that we must connect here: When God speaks, delayed obedience is equal to disobedience. For an easy—and less crucial example (pick your situation)—if your mom asks you to clean your room, your spouse asks you to talk about an issue, or your boss asks you to step into his/her office, which is typically when these people are asking you for action:

A—now, or

B—in a few hours, or

C—if you get to it, maybe sometime next week?

Likely A, maybe B, but certainly not C. Why should God be any different? God's work is important and often people's lives and eternities may be hanging in the balance.

> *Then someone said to Jesus, "I want to go with you, Lord, but first let me go back and take care of things at home." Jesus answered, "Anyone who starts plowing and keeps looking back isn't worth a thing to God's kingdom!" (Luke 9:57–62, CEV)*

This man was similar to the second one in that he wanted to go back home, take care of some business, and tell everyone goodbye. The analogy Jesus uses is a practical one, because the terrain in that area was often rocky and hilly, so looking back while plowing could be dangerous to the farmer and detrimental to the animal and equipment. A farmer had to keep his eyes fixed forward on the horizon to plow in a straight line and also to watch the path to avoid rocks, holes, and even cliffs.

The point of Jesus' analogy: God's Kingdom is always moving forward, never looking back.

EXCUSES OR EXAMPLES

Now, let's contrast these people to Jesus' original disciples. Watch for the difference . . .

> *While Jesus was walking along the shore of Lake Galilee, he saw two brothers. One was Simon, also known as Peter, and the other was Andrew. They were fishermen, and they were casting their net into the lake. Jesus said to them, "Come*

with me! I will teach you how to bring in people instead of fish." Right then the two brothers dropped their nets and went with him. Jesus walked on until he saw James and John, the sons of Zebedee. They were in a boat with their father, mending their nets. Jesus asked them to come with him too. Right away they left the boat and their father and went with Jesus. (Matthew 4:18–22, CEV)

Comparing this passage to the first three we looked at, we see in the first group, men making excuses and in this last group, men making examples. One group dropped some words, while the other dropped their nets. One group faded away, while the other followed on.

See the difference between Watchers and Doers?

Evidently Jesus found some more Doers. Check out Luke 10:1 . . .

Later the Lord chose seventy-two other followers and sent them out two by two to every town and village where he was about to go.

Jesus also gave them His authority to preach His message of salvation and heal the sick. (Luke 10:9) Think of the amazing, once-in-a-lifetime miracles these people were a part of. You can bet there were some hard times and plenty of rejection, but these were the very first Christ followers, operating and living under His authority and power. What an awesome privilege and adventure!

Sadly, think of all that the first group missed out on.

It's time to stop and evaluate these stories from a personal level. What are some excuses you might offer to Jesus? Be honest. Get real. Here's some examples . . .

I want to have some "fun" before anything "serious" starts in my life.

I have to start college, finish college, or graduate school.

I bet my family will stress, so I better wait.

I'm engaged, or I'm planning on getting engaged soon.

I'm expecting a promotion at my job.

I need to get settled into marriage first before we make any major changes.

We need to get the kids raised and then we'll commit to a ministry.

I have to get all my debt paid off first.

I bet my husband/wife will freak, so I should hold off until a better time.

Now—let's be extremely clear here—we are not suggesting you defy any authority, go against any relationship, or shirk any responsibility or commitment. The point is that these are often used as excuses to do nothing or to sound like noble and responsible reasons to not engage God's Kingdom in your life. To explain—many times people who make these excuses will never communicate with parents, spouse, fiance, boss, or children about a calling, but just assume a negative outcome or avoid talking at all, because it just might go quite well and remove the excuse. Make sense? Of course, detailed communication and prayer with those you love should always precede the pursuit of a calling. But we should never use our relationships for our own excuses.

Let's address debt for a moment, since that was one of the excuses listed. For most young people today, there are two areas that are the most likely to create debt—a car and college.

Most of the time, a car loan of $200–300 a month when a young person is working and making a decent wage won't hinder a pursuit of ministry, but it certainly could. The reason going into any kind of debt at a young age may not be wise is because committing to a two to five year loan at this season of life is saddling you with a money demand that could easily affect many decisions—ministry or not.

For example, a young lady decides at the beginning of her senior year of high school that she wants to buy a new car. The interest rate is even 0 percent for 3 years, her dad will co-sign, and she works 20 hours a week at $10 an hour. No problem. She'll have it paid off with no interest by her junior year of college. But near the end of her senior year, her church offers to send her to Africa for the summer to do mission work at an orphanage there. It's her dream situation. But what can she do about the $750 she'll need for the car payment while she's gone and not working? Can God provide that need if she prays for His help? Certainly. But the first question is what was God's will about the car to begin with? That's our focus for this discussion.

See how tricky even a simple debt can become?

Now for the big one—college loans. Sadly, student loan debt has kept many thousands of young people from pursuing ministry and calling. It has kept young couples in their 30s from becoming missionaries, because they still owed $50,000 after being out of school for many years. This book is not a financial counseling resource, so we won't tell you whether or not to incur student loans for school. Our goal is simply to make you aware that debt of any kind can be a hindrance to your freedom in responding to God's call. We simply want to say, seriously think about, pray about, and get wise counsel before incurring any debt.

On the lines below, write down your own *excuses* to just keep watching:

_____
_____
_____
_____
_____

Now, you should be able to see what can, or could, tempt you to just keep watching. You know what your excuses are, or at least could be soon.

REASONS TO SAY YES

Let's turn the corner now to a completely positive, hopeful side. What are, or could be, your *reasons* for saying a full on "yes" to Jesus, to start doing what He asks of you?

Here's your first one.... People. You know, those "God-so-loved, the-harvest-is-ready, we-love-because-He-loved-us-first, least-of-these" people—family, friends, classmates, co-workers, and neighbors who need Him. There are people right now, living without Christ, and you are the absolute best person to reach them and touch their lives with God's truth.

You may think, "Well, God is sovereign, so if I decide to watch and don't reach them, He'll use someone else." Yeah, you're right, depending on your theology, He's God and that's probably true, but who loses on that deal? ... You do. Why? Because just like the three people in the opening passages, you miss out on getting in on the miracles of God.

Know this—He created you to *do*. Not *watch*. Yes, you watch Him at work, but then you join up with Him and participate. That's why He said, 'Come, follow me." He didn't say, "Climb up in the bleachers and cheer." He didn't say, "Stand over there and shut up while I work." He said, "Follow me. Work with me. Get involved with all that I am doing in the world. I want you beside me, sharing the abundant life I bring."

His disciples were right in the middle of healings, water walking, demon casting, food multiplying, sin forgiving, dead resurrecting, temple clearing, teaching, preaching, Pharisee quaking, and culture shaking. The only thing Jesus did alone, without them, was die on the cross. That was the one ministry He didn't invite them to join

Him in. He alone could save mankind, sacrifice His life, and shed royal blood. But that death and blood launched the revolution that they led and we carry on today.

Who is waiting on you right now to stop watching and start doing? Not in a year, or 5 years, or 10 years? Now.

Who could be waiting on you to move, act, speak, work, and engage?

What might you be missing out on?

What amazing work of God might be right around the corner for you?

What once-in-a-lifetime blessing could be yours in just a few short weeks?

Is it time to stop making *excuses*? The ones you have now and the ones you plan on having down the road?

Is it time to start giving *reasons* for joining God on the most incredible adventure you could imagine—the life He mapped out for you while you were still in your mother's womb?

Who doesn't want to change the world? Who wants to just remain status quo? Not you! Realize today there are people that you alone will impact. God has your path destined for people right now and He will use you to change their lives!

You saw me before I was born. Every day of my life was recorded in your book. Every moment was laid out before a single day had passed. (Psalm 139:16, NLT.)

For I know the plans I have for you," says the Lord. "They are plans for good and not for disaster, to give you a future and a hope. (Jeremiah 29:11, NLT)

I pray that Christ Jesus and the church will forever bring praise to God. His power at work in us can do far more than we dare ask or imagine. Amen. (Ephesians 3:21, CEV)

Take a few minutes and on the lines below, prayerfully consider and write down your own reasons to start doing, to begin obeying Him:

_____

_____

_____

_____

_____

PERSONALIZING THE GOSPEL

The entire chapter of John 17 is printed below. It is an amazing passage—an eavesdrop on the door of Heaven. The transcript of Jesus talking to the Father about us. . . . yeah, us!

In light of considering the excuses to throw out and the reasons to press on, prayerfully read Jesus' words.

After Jesus had finished speaking to his disciples, he looked up toward heaven and prayed: Father, the time has come for you to bring glory to your Son, in order that he may bring glory to you. And you gave him power over all people, so that he would give eternal life to everyone you give him. Eternal life is to know you, the only true God, and to know Jesus Christ, the one you sent. I have brought glory to you here on earth by doing everything you gave me to do. Now, Father, give me back the glory that I had with you before the world was created. You have given me some followers from this world, and I have shown them what you are like. They were yours, but you gave them to me, and they have obeyed you. They know that you gave me everything I have. I told my followers what you told me, and they accepted it. They know that I came from you, and they believe that you are the one who sent me. I am praying for them, but not for those who belong to this world. My followers belong to you, and I am praying for them. All that I have is yours, and all that you have is mine, and they will bring glory to me. Holy Father, I am no longer in the world. I am coming to you, but my followers are still in the world. So keep them safe by the power of the name that you have given me. Then they will be one with each other, just as you and I are one. While I was with them, I kept them safe by the power you have given me. I guarded them, and not one of them was lost, except the one who had to be lost. This happened so that what the Scriptures say would come true. I am on my way to you. But I say these things while I am still in the world, so that my followers will have the same complete joy that I do. I have told them your message. But the people of this world hate them, because they don't belong to this world, just as I don't. Father, I don't ask you to take my followers out of the world, but keep them safe from the evil one. They don't belong to this world, and neither do I. Your word is the truth. So let this truth make them completely yours. I am sending them into the world, just as you sent me. I have given myself completely for their sake, so that they may belong completely to the truth. I am not praying just for these followers. I am also praying for everyone else who will have faith because of what my followers will say about me. I want all of them to be one with each other, just as I am one with you and you are one with me. I also want them to be one with us. Then the people of this world will believe that you sent me. I have honored my followers in the same way that you honored me, in order that they may be one with each other, just as we are one. I am one with them, and you are one with me, so that they may become completely one. Then this world's people will know that you sent me. They will know that you love my followers as much as you love me. Father, I want everyone you have given me to be with me, wherever I am. Then they will see the glory that you have given me, because you loved me before the world was created. Good Father, the people of this world don't know you. But I know you, and my followers know that you sent me. I told them what you are like, and I will tell them even more. Then the love that you have for me will become part of them, and I will be one with them.

Isn't that cool?! Jesus was praying for all His followers—that day and the millions out in the future. As a Christian, you are in that number. This passage is about you. To better take this truth in, below is John 17 again, but there are blanks in this version. Go ahead and write your name in each blank, then when you're done, read it again. Whenever you start to struggle with your Christian walk, come back and re-read this. When you wrestle with doing—and you will—re-read this unique and personalized version of John 17.

After Jesus had finished speaking to his disciples, he looked up toward heaven and prayed: Father, the time has come for you to bring glory to your Son, in order that he may bring glory to you. And you gave him power over _____ , so that he would give eternal life to _____. Eternal life is to know you, the only true God, and to know Jesus Christ, the one you sent. I have brought glory to you here on earth by doing everything you gave me to do. Now, Father, give me back the glory that I had with you before the world was created. You have given me _____ from this world, and I have shown _____ what you are like. _____[is]

yours, but you gave _____ to me, and _____ [has] obeyed you. _____ knows that you gave me everything I have. I told _____ what you told me, and _____ accepted it. _____ knows that I came from you, and _____ believes that you are the one who sent me. I am praying for _____ , but not for those who belong to this world. _____ belongs to you, and I am praying for _____ . All that I have is yours, and all that you have is mine, and _____ will bring glory to me. Holy Father, I am no longer in the world. I am coming to you, but _____ [is] still in the world. So keep _____ safe by the power of the name that you have given me. Then [we] will be one with each other, just as you and I are one. While I was with them, I kept them safe by the power you have given me. I guarded them, and not one of them was lost, except the one who had to be lost. This happened so that what the Scriptures say would come true. I am on my way to you. But I say these things while I am still in the world, so that _____ will have the same complete joy that I do. I have told _____ your message. But the people of this world hates _____ , because _____ [doesn't] belong to this world, just as I don't. Father, I don't ask you to take _____ out of the world, but keep _____ safe from the evil one. _____ [doesn't] belong to this world, and neither do I. Your word is the truth. So let this truth make _____ completely yours. I am sending _____ into the world, just as you sent me. I have given myself completely for _____ , so that _____ may belong completely to the truth. I am not praying just for _____ . I am also praying for everyone else who will have faith because of what _____ will say about me. I want all of them to be one with each other, just as I am one with you and you are one with me. I also want them to be one with us. Then the people of this world will believe that you sent me. I have honored _____ in the same way that you honored me, in order that _____ may be one with [the others], just as we are one. I am one with them, and you are one with me, so that they may become completely one. Then this world's people will know that you sent me. They will know that you love as much as you love me. Father, I want everyone you have given me to be with me, wherever I am. Then they will see the glory that you have given me, because you loved me before the world was created. Good Father, the people of this world don't know you. But I know you, and _____ knows that you sent me. I told _____ what you are like, and I will tell _____ even more. Then the love that you have for me will become part of _____ , and I will be one with _____ .

There's just something about personalizing the Gospel that helps us comprehend how deeply personal Christ's love is for us.

One of the most motivating passages of Scripture, to help us as believers keep our eye on the prize, is found in Matthew 25. Jesus tells a parable about a man that is rewarding those who have had stewardship of his money. He explains that the ones who were good stewards, not only will receive rewards, but will hear the master say, "Well done, good and faithful servant!" This passage has long been interpreted that when we enter the Kingdom of Heaven one day, as a follower of Christ and a steward of His work, He will say to me and to you, "Well done, good and faithful servant!"

So ... you in or out? You watching or doing? You walking off or following close? Excuses or reasons? The crowd or Christ? Hey, it is most certainly your call. But we are at the point in the book where it's time to do this thing or put the book away.

LINE IN THE SAND

Author Mike Cox wrote an article entitled "Line in the Sand" about the now famous, somewhat controversial story of the Alamo's Fall. Historians are still debating over whether this story is true. What is irrefutable is that the story of Colonel William Barrett Travis drawing a line in the sand with his sword—be it truth or legend—gave Texas, America, and eventually the world, one of its most enduring metaphors. The line in the sand image has great power, because it represents something that is absolutely true: Making a courageous decision often comes at a high price.

By March 5, 1836, Colonel Travis had known for several days that his situation inside the old Spanish mission called The Alamo had become hopeless. Several thousand soldiers under the command of Mexican General Antonio Lopez de Santa Anna had Travis and some 189 other defenders surrounded.

The young Texas colonel, only 26, was a lawyer, not a professional military man, but Travis knew enough history to understand that in a siege, the army on the outside usually prevails over the army on the inside—especially when they are grossly outnumbered. So he gathered his fellow defenders that Saturday afternoon and gave them a speech.

"We must die," he began. "Our business is not to make a fruitless effort to save our lives, but to choose the manner of our death." Then, with a flourish, Travis drew his sword and slowly marked a line in the Texas sand. "I now want every man who is determined to stay here and die with me to come across this line."

There is another "line in the sand" drawn throughout history for each one of us. On one side of the line is the world saying, "Stay with us and live for today, forget about the future, follow your own heart, for tomorrow we die." Then on the other side stands Jesus, saying, "I died so that you might truly live, so come and pick up your cross, die to yourself, and follow me."

Our hope and prayer—and the only true purpose for these pages—is that you walk across the line to follow Jesus, serve Him with all your heart, soul, body, and mind. And then one day, before the throne of Heaven hear, "Well done, good and faithful servant!"

CHAPTER 6 DISCUSSION QUESTIONS

1. Did you relate to the three people who had excuses or conditions about following Jesus? How? If no, why?

2. How did you feel about Jesus' responses to their excuses?

3. Discuss the phrase "delayed obedience is equal to disobedience." Agree or disagree? Explain.

4. Why do you think the disciples may have been so quick to leave everything to follow Jesus?

5. Discuss the excuses you wrote down—the ones you're comfortable with discussing.

6. How does it affect you to think God may have people right now, or very soon, whom He needs you to reach?

7. Discuss the connection between Psalm 139:16, Jeremiah 29:11, and Ephesians 3:21. How do these verses motivate our obedience?

8. Discuss the reasons that you wrote down to start doing.

9. Did the personalization of John 17 impact you? How?

10. Discuss the "line in the sand" concept. Why do you think so many important things in life come down to making a hard choice?

> **POST/TWEET**
>
> There are people, living without Christ, and you are the absolute best person to reach them with God's truth. #stopwatchingstartdoing

CHAPTER 7

WILL YOU LIVE OUT YOUR CALLING?

We see an amazing transformation in the lives of Jesus' disciples from the day they dropped their nets to after His ascension into Heaven when they are preaching and healing in His name. We see normal men and women daily living out a supernatural lifestyle. What happened to them? The life of Jesus became their life. His way became their way. His truth became their truth. The exact same thing that God wants to do with you.

If your faith is going to be real—not American-cultural-religious-real, but real like the disciples' real—it can't be an item on your weekly to-do list. It's not on your checklist. It is the list!

Think about a waffle. Golden brown with a grid of perfect, little compartments. That is often how we think of our lives. We have our family compartment, friend compartment, school compartment, job compartment, money compartment, fun compartment . . . oh, and the church compartment.

But here comes the syrup, pouring out onto and flowing over it all. Running down into and filling up every compartment, so now you don't see all those divided sections, as much as you see a covered and saturated delicacy. That's a very simple analogy of Jesus covering our lives. He doesn't go neatly into one or two little squares. He soaks, drenches, and floods our entire being.

> *Love God, your God, with your whole heart: love him with all that's in you, love him with all you've got!* (Deuteronomy 6:5, MSG)

A PROMISE FOR DO-ERS

Check out Matthew 6:33, expressed four different ways:

> *But seek first his kingdom and his righteousness, and all these things will be given to you as well.* (NIV)
>
> *But more than anything else, put God's work first and do what he wants. Then the other things will be yours as well.* (CEV)
>
> *Seek the Kingdom of God above all else, and live righteously, and he will give you everything you need.* (NLT)
>
> *Instead, be concerned above everything else with the Kingdom of God and with what he requires of you, and he will provide you with all these other things.* (GNT)

We've given you different versions to let this truth sink in deep. This is a powerful verse, because it contains an amazing promise from God.

Think about this: Why are you still here on the Earth?

If you're a Christian, you believe that when you die, you will have an eternal home in Heaven, right? But God hasn't taken you there yet, so you must have some kind of purpose here right now, something He wants you to do or accomplish before He takes you home. You have your "ticket" to Heaven, but you're on a journey with Him now that has stops and adventures along the way.

In Matthew 6:33, Jesus was teaching to a large crowd, telling them what His Kingdom is all about. Let's take this verse apart to see what He's saying.

SEEK

At the beginning of each version, we see an action verb. Namely "seek," "put," and "be concerned." These words are directed at us, challenging us to "go after, pursue, look for, and prioritize."

Ever played Hide & Seek? What does the Seeker do? If you're seeking something, do you sit around and wait on it to come to you?

No, you go after it. You take action. You're actively searching to find what you seek.

FIRST

Connected to these action verbs are the phrases, "first," "more than anything else," "above all else," and "above everything else."

Do these phrases sound like you should "seek, put, or be concerned with" sometime later on when you can? When you feel like it? When you want to? When everything else is done and you're bored? No, this is the language of priority. First is first. The first thing I do in all things is to seek.

KINGDOM

So, what do you seek or place first? Your kingdom? Your spouse's kingdom? Boyfriend or girlfriend's kingdom? Your parents' kingdom. Your boss' kingdom. No. Whose kingdom? God's.

One of the number one reasons that relationships end—from casual dating to serious ones to engagements to marriage—is when one decides he or she will no longer place the relationship first. One of the primary ways this is expressed is by putting someone else in the place of the one that was once loved and prioritized. Everyone knows where a relationship is going when one says to the other, "Well, I met someone else..."

When one person in the relationship begins to feel like the other's heart is no longer in it, the end is usually near. Here is the incredibly great news about God. He will never say to any of us, "Well, I met someone else..." or "I just don't think this is working out." He is all in 24/7/365 and is constantly pursuing us. He seeks us all the time—forever.

The challenge is for us to remain faithful to Him. Yet when we fail, and we will, we seek forgiveness and move right back into relationship with Him.

Let's review what we've seen in Matthew 6:33 so far: As a follower of Christ, you are to go after, pursue, the very first thing—before anything else—the kingdom of God. That's a very clear mission statement.

Next, let's step back and look at the word "kingdom."

Unlike an earthly king's physical realm, God's kingdom is only visible in the lives of His followers who are doing the very thing we are talking about: Seeking Him first. Placing their relationship with Him before anything else. Doing what He wants them to do. Obeying Him. God's kingdom is His people and His activity that surrounds their lives. Earthly kings have borders and boundaries; God does not.

RIGHTEOUSNESS

Next, we have the phrases, "and his righteousness," "what he wants," "live righteously," and "what he requires of you." So what is righteousness? It is God's way to right, just, and holy living through His Son, Jesus Christ. It is God's way to live. What He wants. What He requires of you.

Whose righteousness is it? Yours? Ours? No. God's. Only His. We have no righteousness of our own. (Romans 3:11) God has made a way for you and me to be right with Him, for us to have a right relationship with a holy God. His name is Jesus—the only Source of righteousness.

GOD GIVES

And, finally, the last part—"and all these things will be given to you as well," "then the other things will be yours as well," "he will give you everything you need," and "he will provide you with all these other things."

For this to fully make sense, we must go back and see what He is referring to when he says "things." Leading up to verse 33, Matthew

6 contains the famous "do not worry" passage. Here it is—verses 25–32:

> *I tell you not to worry about your life. Don't worry about having something to eat, drink, or wear. Isn't life more than food or clothing? Look at the birds in the sky! They don't plant or harvest. They don't even store grain in barns. Yet your Father in heaven takes care of them. Aren't you worth more than birds? Can worry make you live longer? Why worry about clothes? Look how the wild flowers grow. They don't work hard to make their clothes. But I tell you that Solomon with all his wealth wasn't as well clothed as one of them. God gives such beauty to everything that grows in the fields, even though it is here today and thrown into a fire tomorrow. He will surely do even more for you! Why do you have such little faith? Don't worry and ask yourselves, "Will we have anything to eat? Will we have anything to drink? Will we have any clothes to wear?" Only people who don't know God are always worrying about such things. Your Father in heaven knows that you need all of these.* (CEV)

When you seek God's kingdom first and His righteousness, then you won't have to worry about your life. God will take care of you—in every detail.

Think on this question for a moment: Do you know anyone who lets God totally take care of him/her and doesn't seem to worry about the stuff everyone else does? Do you know anyone who is so God-focused that, while his/her life certainly isn't perfect, it is always peaceful? Write down his/her name or names here:

_____

_____

_____

GOD'S UNBREAKABLE PROMISE

The bottom line of this verse is: God is promising you that if you will take care of His business here on earth, He will take care of you here and for eternity. You take care of His kingdom and He'll take care of yours.

Could anyone ever offer you a better deal? Well, some deals certainly sound amazing, but are they really? Let's take a look at pro sports, for example.

Sports Illustrated magazine released some interesting information: "By the time they have been retired for two years, 78 percent of former NFL players have gone bankrupt or are under financial stress. Within five years of retirement, an estimated 60 percent of former NBA players are broke."

> So many people today live with an entitlement attitude toward life, meaning everyone owes them something. So many also struggle with laziness and apathy, always taking the low road in life. Live like anything that anyone does for you is a blessing. Be grateful for all God gives and you will find Him and His righteousness.

What about a movie contract or a record deal? Fox News' Pop Tarts reported, "5 Top Ways Celebrities Lose All Their Cash." Listed were the cases of singer Toni Braxton, rocker Vince Neil, boxer Mike Tyson, actors Wesley Snipes, Nicolas Cage, and Eva Longoria. Even Britney Spears, Jennifer Lopez, and Jay-Z were mentioned for losing big money on failed businesses. The five ways were poor money management skills, bad advice, theft and fraud, drugs and alcohol, and constant overspending.

Here's the other side of that coin . . .

In 2003, Scott Neeson was making over $1 million a year working for Sony Pictures. Prior to that, he worked for 20th Century Fox where he'd overseen the release of blockbuster movies such as *Braveheart, Titanic, Star Wars,* and *X-Men.* The southern California media called him "Mr. Hollywood." He lived in Beverly Hills, owned a yacht, and drove a Porsche. He hung out with movie stars and dated models. Scott Neeson "had it made."

Telling a friend that "there has to be more to life than making movies," he set off on a 5-week trip through Asia. Intending to only stay in Phnom Penh, Cambodia for a few days, Neeson was shocked at the poverty he witnessed there. He went to the city dump where children scavenged for food. He found two girls and promised their mothers $50 a month if they would send the girls to school and no longer make them go to the dump. He recalls asking himself, "Is this all it takes to change the lives of two children?"

Though Neeson went back to the U.S., he committed to return once a month. Within a year, he had rescued 12 homeless children, rented a building to use as a shelter, and hired a small staff to run it 24/7. One day while in Cambodia, trying to decide whether to commit his life fully to the new mission, his cell phone rang. It was a famous movie star client of his.

Hollywood star: "Scott, we have a problem."

Scott: "Well, what is it?"

Hollywood star: "The plane the studio chartered for me doesn't have the right water and food I require. We're not getting on until this is resolved. My life is not supposed to be this difficult. Fix it!"

That was Scott's turning point, because he had also just learned that five of the children in his orphanage had typhoid.

In 2004, he began the Cambodian Children's Fund with his own money and left Hollywood for good. To date, CCF takes care of more than 1,200 children and employs 445 locals. They also have a nursery and day care for another 20 kids. He now comes back to Hollywood only to raise money for his work in Cambodia.

Isn't it funny how so many of us want the life of the movie star in Scott's story, yet Christ is leading us to the life that Scott took on in Cambodia? It's so easy in our culture to get the priorities backwards.

Scott Neeson sensed there had to be more to life. He went seeking and he found. When he did, he stopped watching and started doing. And he also stopped babysitting watchers.

If you cling to your life, you will lose it, and if you let your life go, you will save it. (Luke 17:33, NLT)

IT'S WHO YOU ARE

Take a few minutes and write out how your own calling from God is impacted by God's promise in Matthew 6:33.

_____
_____
_____
_____
_____

Next, take another few minutes and write out what "those things" are for you. Right now, what are your biggest concerns for your life and future?

What do you feel you need God to "add" to you, so you can be free to seek Him first.

_____
_____
_____
_____
_____

Are you beginning to see how God's call on your life to use your gift and passion for Him is not really about what you do, but mostly about who you are. For the disciples, it became who they were. For

Scott Neeson, it became, not a thing he did, but who he now is. It is the same for you.

Christianity is not about what you do, but who you are. Yet, what you do will always flow out of who you are. A life lived following Jesus isn't a to-do list, but an identity. Not a religion, but a relationship.

Who are you? Will you live out who you are?

CHAPTER 7 DISCUSSION QUESTIONS

1. Discuss the waffle analogy. What are some ways that we compartmentalize our lives? How does/why does Jesus saturate all of it?

2. Have you ever thought about the fact that if God has saved you, you can go to Heaven, but since you're here, He must have a purpose for you? Discuss that concept.

3. Why do you think it's so difficult for us to put God first in all things—whether it be a crisis or a celebration, a victory or a failure?

4. As Christians, we are taught early on that we are to follow Christ and be obedient, so why do you think finding someone who seeks Him, His Kingdom, and His righteousness first is so rare these days? Discuss.

5. Why do you think we often strive to be righteous—live right—on our own, rather than rely on Christ and His power?

6. Discuss Matthew 6:25–32. How should this affect our life and our worries?

7. Talk about your thoughts on the last two sentences of that passage: *Only people who don't know God are always worrying about such things. Your Father in heaven knows that you need all of these.*

8. Discuss the sports stats and celebrity failures. Why do you think we tend to only hear about the success stories and the big contracts?

9. Talk about Scott Neeson's story. How does his story inspire you as a believer?

10. Discuss the "Who You Are" sections where you wrote down your thoughts. Share what you're comfortable with sharing.

POST/TWEET

A life lived following Jesus isn't a to-do list, but an identity. Not a religion, but a relationship. #stopwatchingstartdoing

POST/TWEET

Christianity is not about what you do, but who you are. Yet, what you do will always flow out of who you are. #stopwatchingstartdoing

CHAPTER 8

WILL YOU THINK LIKE A DO-ER?

Actually, a better way to title this chapter might be "Will you think like Jesus?" But that gets really intimidating—fast. So, in keeping with our title and theme, that's why we're saying, "think like a do-er." And yet, Jesus was the ultimate Do-er.

All actions start in the mind. Your body can't do anything that you don't "think" first. Even an involuntary action, such as a cough or sneeze, moves through your brain first. It's the information and message center for the body, like an air traffic control tower. So, we're dedicating an entire chapter to this new way of thinking that you're going to have to engage in, if you're going to stop watching and start doing.

Have you ever heard of Bible Drill? Some of you may have taken part in this activity at your church. Bible Drill is a competition where the participants try to find a Bible verse faster than their opponents. There are city, regional, and even national competitions. A working knowledge of the Bible's books and sequence is essential to compete. When a participant hears the verse or passage to find and hears the "go," an immediate mental map of the books, then chapters, and verses is a must to win.

Here's a question to ponder: Is it possible that a Bible Drill winner might not be a Christian? Well, certainly. They just need to have information memorized, which doesn't require faith to do. Is it possible that a Bible Drill winner might not have a strong understanding and application of Scripture? Absolutely. Again, they could just be great at mental organization and applying a system.

Let's be clear—Bible Drill is an awesome tool to help young people know the books of the Bible and have a solid, working knowledge of God's Word. The point of this illustration is to see that a working knowledge of the Bible doesn't mean the truth is applied. It has to move to action to change your life. Our knowledge has to translate into forward movement.

A BELIEF SYSTEM

To communicate this next point, let's first define a term—Belief System. A belief system is a mental and spiritual state of mind from which you derive some or all of your rules and principles for living. A belief system could be a philosophy or a religion. Typically, it involves some kind of god, but may just be a manner of how to think and approach life. In fact, atheism—the belief that there is no god—and agnostic—someone who is neutral to the concept of a god—are belief systems. The bottom line is it is information that you regularly call on in your life, by which you live your life.

In all the belief systems that have ever existed before, exist now, and will ever exist, there are some common truths. As a non-believer of any belief system, you are ignorant of the necessary knowledge needed to be enlightened. So, you must hear and receive the information, which is then either rejected or received.

Reception of that information can become revelation—the full acceptance of the belief system as personal truth.

Reception ends the ignorance. Revelation begins the belief... Let's repeat that... Reception ends the ignorance... Revelation begins the belief. Most belief systems end here. Once you have received and accepted the information and are enlightened, you are in the club!

To simplify...

The choice: rejection or reception.

Reception can bring revelation.

Revelation brings belief.

Belief brings more reception.

And so on.

But Jesus came along and added another step, a new step. What was it? . . . Obedience. Obedience that produces application.

Think about this: How do you know if something is true in your life or even someone else's? Can you see belief? Can you see knowledge? Of course not. You see obedience. The action followed from the motivation of the belief. You see the knowledge carried out into movement.

Here's an analogy: A young man meets a young woman. They begin to hang out. They spend more and more time together. At some point, both of them experience love. What if the young man just kept his love for the young lady to himself? He thinks it. He feels it. He believes it. But there will come a point where the love that he feels will drive him to the revelation that this is the girl for him. His belief drives his behavior to action. He expresses his love and asks her to marry him. Everyone around the couple now believes they love each other. Why? Because the actions have proven the revelation. I know that all sounds terribly un-romantic, but it's the logic behind love and everyone knows about love.

IGNORANCE TO KNOWLEDGE TO APPLICATION

James expressed the concept of ignorance to application perfectly.

But don't just listen to God's word. You must do what it says. Otherwise, you are only fooling yourselves. For if you listen to the word and don't obey, it is like glancing at your face in a mirror. You see yourself, walk away, and forget what you look like. But if you look carefully into the perfect law that sets you free, and if you do what it says and don't forget what you heard, then God will bless you for doing it. (James 1:22–25, NLT)

So, Christianity became the first and only belief system that requires another step past knowledge, past revelation.

Doing what is right and fair pleases the Lord more than an offering. (Proverbs 21:3, CEV)

> Application slows discipleship way down. Just gaining knowledge can move things along quickly. But a life of character and integrity will take years to produce. A godly life will not happen overnight. Be patient and press on! One obedient decision at a time.

Do you see how this added step of action demands much more of your life than just accepting a set of truths? Can you see how this requires you to think differently than just being a religious person who follows certain rules?

Does this mean everyone who claims to be a Christian will move to application? No. This is where we get the Watchers.

Is it possible that many more people stop at having the knowledge of Christ, yet never move toward true obedience and application? Of course.

For many, many years, a common statistic given in regards to any organization is that 20 percent of the people involved do 80 percent of the work. This certainly applies to most of the church today. Why? Because people stop at knowledge without application. Which is exactly why so many belief systems stop there too!

Watchers that move to Do-ers are those that move from ignorance to knowledge to application.

In Chapter 6, we referred to Matthew 25, but now let's look deeper at it, applying what we have learned thus far in this chapter.

Verses 31–46—When the Son of Man comes in his glory with all of his angels, he will sit on his royal throne. The people of all nations will be brought before him, and he will separate them, as shepherds separate their sheep from their goats. He will place the sheep on his right and the goats on his left. Then the king will say to those on his right, "My father has blessed you! Come and receive the kingdom that was prepared for you before the world was created. When I was hungry, you gave me something to eat, and when I was thirsty, you gave me something to drink. When I was a stranger, you welcomed me, and when I was naked, you gave me clothes to wear. When I was sick, you took care of me, and when I was in jail, you visited me." Then the ones who pleased the Lord will ask, "When did we give you something to eat or drink? When did we welcome you as a stranger or give you clothes to wear or visit you while you were sick or in jail?" The king will answer, "Whenever you did it for any of my people, no matter how unimportant they seemed, you did it for me." Then the king will say to those on his left, "Get away from me! You are under God's curse. Go into the everlasting fire prepared for the devil and his angels! I was hungry, but you did not give me anything to eat, and I was thirsty, but you did not give me anything to drink. I was a stranger, but you did not welcome me, and I was naked, but you did not give me any clothes to wear. I was sick and in jail, but you did not take care of me." Then the people will ask, "Lord, when did we fail to help you when you were hungry or thirsty or a stranger or naked or sick or in jail?" The king will say to them, "Whenever you failed to help any of my people, no matter how unimportant they seemed, you failed to do it for me." Then Jesus said, "Those people will be punished forever. But the ones who pleased God will have eternal life."

Notice that the "goats"—those who *did not* minister in Jesus' name—asked, "When were you in that predicament and we missed it?" While the "sheep"—those who *did* minister in Jesus' name—evidently were so into doing these things and it was such normal activity for them that it didn't stand out to them as anything special.

While at a quick scan these might sound like very similar responses, they couldn't be more opposite. One had to ask when these events even happened, while the other had to be reminded that their normal activity was unique to the world.

Again we see the difference between Watchers and Do-ers. But here, it is clearly painted as the difference between going to Heaven and Hell.

Let's stop here and drive home a very crucial point.

AMAZING GRACE

You can't write a book like this that focuses on action the way we have, constantly using the word "doing," without having some people make accusations that we are making works a part of salvation. We want to make it abundantly clear that we don't believe in Jesus + Anything = Salvation. It is Christ and Christ alone Who saves. Good works don't save us. Hard work doesn't save us. Working "for God" doesn't save us. It is God's Spirit drawing us and we respond in faith. But let's go deeper . . .

Only Jesus has the power to save! His name is the only one in all the world that can save anyone. (Acts 4:12, CEV)

The Holy Spirit alone draws us to salvation. We do not "find" God or Jesus. He is not lost; we are! He alone seeks, finds, and saves us.

For the Son of Man came to seek and save those who are lost." (Luke 19:10, NLT)

What is an appropriate response to being found and saved for Eternity? What do we do after being miraculously rescued from Hell? We respond in worship and obedience. We become do-ers in and of Him Who has saved us, because we have been given the power and the privilege to join God in both relationship and activity.

WILL YOU ACT LIKE A DO-ER?

God has done it all! He sent Christ to make peace between himself and us, and he has given us the work of making peace between himself and others. What we mean is that God was in Christ, offering peace and forgiveness to the people of this world. And he has given us the work of sharing his message about peace. We were sent to speak for Christ, and God is begging you to listen to our message. We speak for Christ and sincerely ask you to make peace with God. (2 Corinthians 5:18–20, CEV)

We do nothing to receive salvation except to express faith in Christ. Jesus alone saves. We then respond to His amazing and free gift by submitting in obedience to Him. A Christ follower is saved by grace—unmerited favor—and through that grace is able to join the Heavenly Father in His Kingdom work.

Anytime anyone attempts to attach anything to Christ for salvation, it is un-Biblical and not of the Truth. So, it is Jesus = Salvation, never Jesus + X = Salvation. Our obedience, action, and doing are simply a response to being saved.

Moving on now, since this chapter is about thinking like a Do-er, consider these passages:

Understanding your word brings light to the minds of ordinary people. (Psalm 119:130)

Jesus answered: Love the Lord your God with all your heart, soul, and mind. (Matthew 22:37, CEV)

The apostles often met together and prayed with a single purpose in mind. (Acts 1:14, CEV)

If our minds are ruled by our desires, we will die. But if our minds are ruled by the Spirit, we will have life and peace. (Romans 8:6, CEV)

Set your minds on things above, not on earthly things. (Colossians 3:2, NIV)

Finally, my friends, keep your minds on whatever is true, pure, right, holy, friendly, and proper. Don't ever stop thinking about what is truly worthwhile and worthy of praise. (Philippians 4:8, CEV)

The mind of Christ in us will produce the actions of Christ!

CHAPTER 8 DISCUSSION QUESTIONS

1. Why is it so crucial to learn to think differently as a Christian?

2. Why is it important that our faith not stop at knowledge?

3. Do you agree that *everyone* lives their lives based on a belief system? Why or why not?

4. Discuss the concept of: Rejection versus Reception. Reception can bring Revelation. Revelation brings Belief.

5. Discuss James 1:22–25.

6. Why do you think Jesus emphasized application of God's truth?

7. Why do you think so many Christians just stop and watch? What stops them from moving on to being do-ers?

8. Discuss Matthew 25—the sheep and goats analogy that Jesus gave.

9. Why is it so important that we not attach anything to a requirement for salvation—other than a relationship with Jesus?

10. What is the difference in being a do-er out of a heart of worship and obedience and being one who strives for God's approval and acceptance?

> **POST/TWEET**
>
> A Christ follower is saved by grace, and through that grace, can join the Heavenly Father in His Kingdom work. #stopwatchingstartdoing

CHAPTER 9

WILL YOU ACT LIKE A DO-ER?

It's interesting that we rarely hear of pastors and teachers connecting the spiritual gifts passages in Romans 12 and 1 Corinthians 12 to Galatians 5:22–23a—the fruit of the Spirit. Most of the teaching on these two topics tends to stay separated, but as you'll see in this chapter, there is a definite and obvious connection.

Let's begin with defining spiritual fruit in this context. Fruit is the end result or product of an effort or mindset. It can be a bad or good outcome, as we'll see, just as fruit on a tree can be edible or rotten.

But the Holy Spirit produces this kind of fruit in our lives: love, joy, peace, patience, kindness, goodness, faithfulness, gentleness, and self-control. (NLT)

Here's why there should be a connection between the gifts and the fruit—if we do the right thing in the wrong way, people can miss the right thing that we do! For example . . .

Someone has the gift of evangelism, but they are extremely impatient with people. "I want you to accept Jesus. Right now!"

Someone has the gift of service, but struggles with joy and peace. They may be dealing with constant stress over problems in the places where they serve. "Why can't they just let me do things the way I want them to be done?!"

Someone has the gift of administration and works hard for their church, but isn't known for being kind and gentle. "I know that you were at the hospital with a member all night, but that's why we pay you. I need your budget report on my desk today!"

Someone has the gift of pastoring, but has an issue with faithfulness and self-control. "I'm calling to tell you that the pastor can't make his appointment with you today. He double-booked again and will get back with you to set another time."

See it? The weakness in the fruit of the spirit can often overshadow and undermine the use of the person's gift. But to the contrary, when we experience someone who consistently expresses a growing level of love, joy, peace, patience, kindness, goodness, faithfulness, gentleness, and self-control to the people around them, we will often allow grace and excuse a weakness in a gift, because of the heart of the person.

How many times have we said, or heard, statements like . . .

"He's not a great preacher, but he's just so full of joy when he speaks, that we love listening to him."

"She may not get as much done as the others, but she has such a peaceful, patient attitude and we love having her around. It's contagious."

"We might could find a better teacher for that class, but his kind and gentle spirit are what draws people to come anyway."

See it here as well? Of course, we want excellence in the Kingdom of God, but people who exude the character of Christ often speak far louder by their actions than better communicators or leaders. Who we are in our character makes a difference in what we do and how we do things.

Now, of course, we are all sinners and are going to consistently make mistakes. However, this passage in Galatians inspires and challenges us in how we are to act toward others. We must realize that behaving as Jesus would is just as important to God as doing the work of Jesus. We can't truly do the work of God if we're acting like the devil!

Over the past several decades, the media has had a heyday with Christian leaders who are doing the "work" of God, yet not in a manner that reflects His character. They love to show men and women that preach to thousands, yet aren't exhibiting the fruit of

God's Spirit. This has continually hurt the church in monumental ways. Which is exactly why we decided to include this passage and topic in this book—for Christianity, the way we behave is just as crucial as the ministry we do.

Let's repeat that last sentence for emphasis—for Christianity, the way we behave is just as crucial as the ministry we do.

Let's expand now and look deeper at this passage.

> So I say, let the Holy Spirit guide your lives. Then you won't be doing what your sinful nature craves. The sinful nature wants to do evil, which is just the opposite of what the Spirit wants. And the Spirit gives us desires that are the opposite of what the sinful nature desires. These two forces are constantly fighting each other, so you are not free to carry out your good intentions. But when you are directed by the Spirit, you are not under obligation to the law of Moses. (v. 16–18, CEV)

One evening, an elder Cherokee chief told his grandson about the greatest battle he had ever fought. He said, "My son, the battle is between two wolves inside us all. One is evil. It is anger, envy, jealousy, greed, arrogance, self-pity, guilt, resentment, lies, pride, and ego. The other is good. It is joy, peace, love, hope, humility, kindness, empathy, generosity, truth, compassion, and faith.

The grandson thought a moment, then asked his grandfather, "So which wolf wins?" The old chief simply answered, "The one you feed."

The chief's answer and verse 18 are directly connected. Living life under the submission and direction of the Holy Spirit will accomplish two things:

1. You will discover, grow, and function in your spiritual gift or gifts.
2. You will grow, mature, and increase in the fruit of God's Spirit.

Each day, we all make the choice of which wolf to feed, which nature to show, and which spiritual force will win. When the sinful nature wins one day, our gift and fruit go unused. But when our "good intentions" (v. 17) mix with God directions, our gift and fruit will show.

Remember these three points from chapter 3? Let's apply them here as well.

When we operate fully in our gifts and passion, and display the [fruit of the Spirit,] then . . .

1. *God is most glorified.*
2. *You are most satisfied.*
3. *The world will be most notified.*

To sum up verses 16–18, God's Spirit is always ready to work in and through us. When we simply submit—allow Him the freedom to work in and around us—God is glorified, we are satisfied, and the world is notified.

> *When you follow the desires of your sinful nature, the results are very clear: sexual immorality, impurity, lustful pleasures, idolatry, sorcery, hostility, quarreling, jealousy, outbursts of anger, selfish ambition, dissension, division, envy, drunkenness, wild parties, and other sins like these. Let me tell you again, as I have before, that anyone living that sort of life will not inherit the Kingdom of God. (v. 19–21 CEV)*

Of course, we all understand and know this list of sins very well. No explanation needed. While you likely haven't committed them all, you have surely struggled with some. The result of going down the road of our own desires ends up at this destination.

This list—the fruit of the flesh— is the result of living a selfish life, just like the other list—the fruit of the Spirit—is the result of living a God-centered life. But we need to point out an extreme difference in these two lists. For the sins listed above, you can choose to do any one of these at any time or you can choose to engage in several. This fruit, these desires, operate individually and exclusively of each other. For example, you can exhibit anger without being lustful; you can be jealous without being drunk; you can cause division without being sexually immoral.

But God's fruit works together and in cooperation with each other. When you show love, you are being peaceful. When you're exhibiting peace, you are showing goodness; when you are being kind, you are showing love. They all work and grow together. Certainly you will be stronger in some than others, but strengthening in one strengthens the others!

The selfish fruit fits with the character of Satan, while the Spirit's fruit fits with the character of Christ. The final word on these verses (v. 21)—someone who consistently acts like this and goes deeper into this behavior won't be involved in God's Kingdom—now or in Eternity.

Next, let's look closer at the fruit of the Spirit. To do this, knowing that Christ is the manifestation of God in the flesh, we will define them using Christ as the focus.

But the Holy Spirit produces this kind of fruit in our lives: love, joy, peace, patience, kindness, goodness, faithfulness, gentleness, and self-control. (v. 22–23a, CEV)

LOVE—caring from the soul of Jesus.

God's very nature and essence expressed in action

Most people think of love as an emotion, and often, culturally, it is. However, Scripture defines God as Love. For a Christian to express love in a Biblical sense, it is far more than just feeling an emotion; it is displaying God's character in action that brings His Kingdom from Heaven to Earth.

We love because God loved us first. (1 John 4:19, CEV)

In Matthew 25 (that we've discussed before), Jesus separates the sheep from the goats—an analogy to those who are His true followers versus those who are not—by those who expressed acts of love to people in need. Once again, His character expressed in action.

While we may say that we love a person, we love chocolate, we love sports, etc., the definition has to be different when connecting to our faith and what this word truly means.

Throughout this chapter, at the end of each definition, we're going to ask you to write someone's name out in the margin that you feel BEST exemplifies this fruit.

Write the name of one person, out in the margin, whom you feel most represents the <u>love</u> of God to you.

JOY—feeling from the heart of Jesus.

We gauge much of our lives on what makes us happy. We make decisions, make plans, start relationships, buy stuff, and work hard to make us feel happiness. The problem is that this is fully dependent upon certain circumstances to begin, sustain, and continue. Joy goes far past being happy.

Happiness is a state of mind, while joy is a mindset.
Happiness comes and goes, while joy can be constant.
Happiness is dependent, while joy is independent.
Happiness is conditional, while joy is unconditional.

You make known to me the path of life; you will fill me with joy in your presence, with eternal pleasures at your right hand. (Psalm 16:11, NIV)

What makes one person happy doesn't make someone else feel the same. Having two hours to read a book makes some people very happy, while someone else would be miserable in ten minutes doing that.

Joy looks the same in every heart. Certainly, some people will express it differently, according to personality, but there is no mistaking joy on any face.

Happiness becomes almost impossible to feel when life is going badly. Joy cannot only be felt at any time, but is actually strengthened when life is challenging.

> *Then Jesus told them this parable: "Suppose one of you has a hundred sheep and loses one of them. Doesn't he leave the ninety-nine in the open country and go after the lost sheep until he finds it? And when he finds it, he joyfully puts it on his shoulders and goes home. Then he calls his friends and neighbors together and says, 'Rejoice with me; I have found my lost sheep.' I tell you that in the same way there will be more rejoicing in heaven over one sinner who repents than over ninety-nine righteous persons who do not need to repent.* (Luke 15:3-7, NIV)

Joy is what we feel when the lost is found!

Remember as happiness moves in and out of your life that joy can grow as you express the heart of Christ to a lost world.

(Write the name of one person in the margin whom you feel most represents the joy of Christ to you.)

PEACE—having the mind of Jesus.

> *Then, because you belong to Christ Jesus, God will bless you with peace that no one can completely understand. And this peace will control the way you think and feel.* (Philippians 4:7, CEV)

If you ask most people to define peace, you will likely hear what it is not, as in "the absence of war" or "when no conflict is present." The issue with these definitions is that peace is not an exchangeable quality that only exists in the default of ending war or trouble. Actually, peace is the stability that has to be present to successfully get us through war, trouble, and dissension.

We find three key points in this verse about peace.

1. True peace, alive in the soul, can only exist if "you belong to Christ Jesus." It is only and exclusively found inside a relationship with Him. He alone is the Source and Sustainer of peace.

2. Peace, by its very nature, is unexplainable. It is most present when it shouldn't be present at all! Peace is most felt when life all around us is at war. Peace comes when it is needed, like the warrior on the white horse coming over the hill, just when things look grim. Such is God's peace. We can't describe it; we can't explain it; and we certainly can't manufacture it on our own.

3. When peace is our soul's foundation, the walls of our life will be stable. It will steady and maintain our thoughts, emotions, attitudes, and feelings. If you daily surrender to Christ, when life deals you a knockout punch, peace will keep you on your feet.

"[May] the Lord turn his face toward you and give you peace." (Numbers 6:26, NIV)

For the Christ follower, peace is not the absence of anything; it is the presence of Jesus!

(Write the name of one person in the margin whom you feel most represents the peace of God to you.)

PATIENCE—waiting quietly on God's timing.

Notice the definition says, "waiting quietly," not loudly. Many people are very vocal about waiting on God. That's clearly not patience.

Ever notice when you hear someone talk about patience these days, it is typically in the context of *not* having patience or losing patience? We say things like, "You're trying my patience," "My patience is wearing thin," or "I'm just about out of patience with him." So many of our uses of the word "patience" really communicate our level of impatience!

In our increasingly high-speed, instant-crazed culture, patience can seem like a dying art and is most certainly losing its true meaning. Where patience might have, at one time, meant waiting days in some settings, it now means minutes.

Here's the tough thing about patience in our Christian journey: the only way that God can teach it to us, and grow us in it, is to give us circumstances where we must wait on Him—patiently. All too often, we get tired of waiting and start trying to "make things happen." But whatever we try to force, will never be as good as what God unfolds.

The Lord isn't slow about keeping his promises, as some people think he is. In fact, God is patient, because he wants everyone to turn from sin and no one to be lost. (2 Peter 3:9, CEV)

At the root of impatience is mistrust. If we don't feel that someone will act on our behalf, we take action on our own. If we trust someone, we will wait on him/her to act.

Having patience means growing in our trust of God, His ways, His timing, and His outcome. When we are impatient, we are also exhibiting pride—the sense that we can do something better on our own.

Finishing is better than starting. Patience is better than pride. (Ecclesiastes 7:8, NLT)

Waiting on God will always bring the strongest finish. Patience is a spiritual muscle that will only be strengthened by waiting on Him. It brings the power to see circumstances as He sees them.

(Write the name of one person in the margin whom you feel most represents God's <u>patience</u> to you.)

KINDNESS—showing the love of Jesus.

Kindness is the outward expression of God's love. Kindness is how true love looks. We hear people say, "She has such a kind face." But the only way we can know for certain that someone is kind is when they show it.

A popular slogan and bumper sticker a few years ago read, "Commit a random act of kindness today." A play on words from "a random act of violence." But just as violence has to be committed to be true violence, so goes kindness in being expressed.

This national news story gives us a great example.

Raymond Mitchell, a 73-year-old clerk at a supermarket was shocked when a young man walked up and handed him an envelope with $50, saying, "This comes from Mr. Hal Reichle, who has appreciated your service for a long time."

The grocery bagger was targeted by SSSSH, the initials for "Secret Society of Serendipitous Service to Hal." The group honors Hal Reichle, an Army helicopter pilot who died at 27 years old during Operation Desert Storm. Hal painted homes while families were on vacation, snuck groceries onto front porches, and once persuaded a banker to give a car loan to a needy pal. Known for his contagious generosity, the soldier inspired these acts of kindness—in Reichle's name, not their own.

To be a part of SSSSH, reports Roger Cram, Reichle's close friend and now the informal head of the group, one must perform an anonymous good deed and describe it in a letter to him. "No signature or return address on the letters or else we throw them away," he insists. "One person used a disability check to buy refreshments for work-release prisoners who were cutting grass and another from someone who bought cable TV for a paraplegic."

The young man who surprised Mitchell said, "It's all very exciting. I've never had more fun than I had giving him that envelope."

What if Roger Cram had said, "Let's get some people together once a month and talk about all that Hal did for others. Let's study his good deeds and remind each other of how cool it was that he did those things." What if they never went outside the walls of the meeting room? Well, first, the group probably wouldn't have stayed active very long and they certainly wouldn't have inspired a news story. The fact that they chose to *do something* in Hal's memory and name not only honors him, but inspires others to continue his legacy.

How much more did Jesus do and how much more should we be doing in His name? This is where the kindness of Christ can make a huge difference in people's lives—through us expressing this fruit in His name.

Let's don't work to simply be kind people; but be accused of being like Jesus through kindness.

(Write the name of one person in the margin whom you feel most represents God's <u>kindness</u> to you.)

GOODNESS—having the motives of Jesus.

Like peace, goodness is a quality that is more about a state of the soul, where the behavior comes from. Goodness influences our mind and heart, flowing out of our attitudes and actions.

As we mentioned earlier in the "two wolves" illustration, there is a constant battle going on in us. Every decision we make is born in our souls. The embryo from which all decisions grow is called a motive. Think about a murder scene. The police stake off the area; they make the chalk lines around the body and begin to scour everything for clues and evidence. But quickly, the detectives are looking for one major thing—the strongest motive to murder this person. Who would have wanted this person dead? The search begins for motive. Why? Because the end result may be murder, but the motive may have been anger, money, jealousy, cover-up, and so on.

We can do something that looks very nice, very good, and even harmless, but we may do it with the wrong motive. We give someone a public compliment, but the motive is manipulation. We buy someone something they want, but our real goal is to get them to do something for us that is more valuable than the item we gave them. Honest appearances can disguise very dishonest motives.

Real godly living is driven by God-fueled motives, which makes for true goodness. What is it that drove Christ in the Garden, throughout the trials, the beatings, the whipping with the cat-of-nine-tails, the walk up to Golgotha with the cross, the nails through the wrists, the nails through the feet, and the hours in agony trying not to suffocate hanging on the cross? What drove Him to give up His life to the Father as a final sacrifice for all sin? . . . The answer: His motive of goodness for you and I!

All we can be capable of in our sin, death, and flesh is more sin, death, and flesh. We are not able to produce life, love, joy, peace, patience, kindness, goodness, gentleness, or self-control. We cannot have pure motives, attitudes, or actions in our own power and strength. Christ offers the opportunity to change all that. God knows the root of our actions is our motives—so He is after our motives. To make them His; To make them pure; To radically change us from the inside out; To make all things new.

> *We have everything we need to live a life that pleases God. It was all given to us by God's own power, when we learned that he had invited us to share in his wonderful goodness. (2 Peter 1:3, CEV)*

Goodness is God giving us what we could never have earned. We display goodness when we serve and love from that same heart of grace and mercy.

(Write the name of one person in the margin whom you feel most represents God's goodness to you.)

FAITHFULNESS—expressing the loyalty of Jesus.

The typical picture most of us think of in regards to faithfulness is marriage. We often hear people say, "She has remained faithful to her husband, no matter what he did" or "He was faithful to her for 35 years." We understand it to mean a deep commitment and care that one person has for another that is reliable, constant, and authentic. Yet, we know that for decades, anyone who is married has a 50 percent chance of failure, and in 100 percent of those situations, a lack of faithfulness will be involved on some level.

When we read the Old Testament, we see God's fierce faithfulness to His people. Even in periods where they could not see His hand, He was working on their behalf. Throughout the Gospels, we see Jesus' unwavering loyalty to and focus on His Father. He exhibited what faithfulness looks like 100 percent of the time.

Faithfulness is also described throughout Jesus' teaching as a treasured and respected quality.

> *The kingdom is also like what happened when a man went away and put his three servants in charge of all he owned. The man knew what each servant could do. So he handed five thousand coins to the first servant, two thousand to the second, and one thousand to the third. Then he left the country. As soon as the man had gone, the servant with the five thousand coins used them to earn five thousand more. The servant who had two thousand coins did the same with his money and earned two thousand more. But the servant with one thousand coins dug a hole and hid his master's money in the ground. Some time later the master of those servants returned. He called them in and asked what they had done with his money. The servant who had been given five thousand coins brought them in with the five thousand that he had earned. He said, "Sir, you gave me five thousand*

coins, and I have earned five thousand more." "Wonderful!" his master replied. "You are a good and faithful servant. I left you in charge of only a little, but now I will put you in charge of much more. Come and share in my happiness!" Next, the servant who had been given two thousand coins came in and said, "Sir, you gave me two thousand coins, and I have earned two thousand more." "Wonderful!" his master replied. "You are a good and faithful servant. I left you in charge of only a little, but now I will put you in charge of much more. Come and share in my happiness!" (Matthew 25:14–23, CEV)

There are two expressions of faithfulness for us to grow and mature in. First is in our relationship with God. Remaining faithful to Him, His Word, and His principles throughout our lives is a journey few will take.

Secondly, showing faithfulness in our relationships. Being known as a reliable, trustworthy, and loyal person that keeps his/her promises is not only an amazing witness for Christ, but the best way to live as well.

We know that we can accept God's Word without question. Our goal is for Him to know us as people whose word can be accepted without question as well.

(Write the name of one person in the margin whom you feel most represents God's faithfulness to you.)

GENTLENESS—having the character of Christ.

In many cultures, gentleness is often seen as weakness. In reality, the Biblical definition of gentleness is controlled strength. Don't think lamb, but lion. For example, if a horse is considered gentle, is it no longer a large animal weighing over 1,000 pounds, capable of running away with you, and kicking you to death? Of course it is. But gentleness means the horse chooses to allow his power and strength to be controlled. Strength submitted is gentleness.

WILL YOU ACT LIKE A DO-ER?

Christ was God—fully contained in a man's body. Was he still able to create, work miracles, heal, forgive sin, stop storms, and cast out demons? Of course. But the power and strength of God was packed into a man under 200 pounds... Amazing.

Read these verses about gentleness, thinking about the character of Christ. This quality is quite obviously given as a sign of godliness.

> Be completely humble and <u>gentle</u>; be patient, bearing with one another in love. (Ephesians 4:2, NIV)

> Let your <u>gentleness</u> be evident to all. The Lord is near. (Philippians 4:5, NIV)

> Therefore, as God's chosen people, holy and dearly loved, clothe yourselves with compassion, kindness, humility, <u>gentleness</u> and patience. (Colossians 3:12, NIV)

> Now the overseer is to be above reproach, faithful to his wife, temperate, self-controlled, respectable, hospitable, able to teach, not given to drunkenness, not violent but <u>gentle</u>, not quarrelsome, not a lover of money. (1 Timothy 3:2-3, NIV)

> Specifically for men: But you, man of God, flee from all this, and pursue righteousness, godliness, faith, love, endurance and <u>gentleness</u>. (1 Timothy 6:11, NIV)

> Specifically for women: Rather, it should be that of your inner self, the unfading beauty of a <u>gentle</u> and quiet spirit, which is of great worth in God's sight. (1 Peter 3:4, NIV)

Receive this new Biblical connotation of being gentle as being like Jesus—strength submitted to the power of God and controlled by the Spirit of God.

(Write the name of one person in the margin whom you feel most represents God's <u>gentleness</u> to you.)

SELF-CONTROL—surrendering your will to God's power

Maybe a better way to define this word is to redefine it as God-control, because that's exactly what self-control for the Christian means. Our sin proves we can't control our own behavior, but when we surrender to God's will and power, He can work in and through us.

Scripture uses multiple analogies of our self-control compared to the protective walls of a city, which in those days meant the difference in a nation or a people standing strong or being defeated by the enemy.

A person without self-control is like a city with broken-down walls. (Proverbs 25:28, NLT)

Better to be patient than powerful; better to have self-control than to conquer a city. (Proverbs 16:32, NLT)

Scripture also tells us that self-control is a quality of a godly leader.

So an elder must be a man whose life is above reproach. He must be faithful to his wife. He must exercise <u>self-control</u>, live wisely, and have a good reputation. (1 Timothy 3:2, NLT)

In the same way, their wives must be respected and must not slander others. They must exercise <u>self-control</u> and be faithful in everything they do. (1 Timothy 3:11, NLT)

Self-control is yielding to God's power to do the things we should—and not do the things we shouldn't.

And, finally, Paul recognizes self-control as an important aspect of our surrender in being fully used by God and boldly sharing Him.

So I ask you to make full use of the gift that God gave you when I placed my hands on you. Use it well. God's Spirit doesn't make cowards out of us. The Spirit gives us power, love, and <u>self-control</u>. Don't be ashamed to speak for our Lord. (2 Timothy 1:6–8a, CEV)

(Write the name of one person in the margin whom you feel most represents God's <u>self-control</u> to you.)

As you grow in Christ, you will grow in the fruit of the Spirit. As you mature in faith, these nine qualities will expand throughout your life. An analogy to explain this process would be: when you are growing up as a child, do your legs grow in proportion to your arms? Of course. Does your head grow in proportion to your feet? Again, yes.

While you will always be stronger in some fruit than others, i.e. better at being peaceful than patient or more patient than peaceful, growing in Christ also grows your capacity to love, have joy, have peace, be patient, be kind, show goodness, be gentle, and have self-control. But the converse is true as well. If you begin to fall away from your faith and start to stray from Christ, your fruit will diminish. But at that point, you will also care less about using your spiritual gifts as well.

We felt it was important to spend a dedicated chapter pointing out the connection between the gifts of the Spirit to the fruit of the Spirit. It makes sense that our behavior and demeanor of being like Jesus would work together in cooperation with the deeds and works He asks us to do; to do the right thing in the right way; to do Jesus things in Jesus' way.

From this day forward, we pray you will always connect your gift to your fruit and your fruit to your gift. We also pray that you grow in them all to be like Christ, doing His will.

CHAPTER 9 DISCUSSION QUESTIONS

1. Discuss this statement: "For Christianity, the way we behave is just as crucial as the ministry we do." How have you seen this to be true?

2. Talk about the Cherokee chief/wolves story. How does this impact your own life?

3. Discuss the "fruit of the flesh" (verses 19–21) versus the "fruit of the Spirit" (verses 22–23a) concept. The character of Satan versus the character of Christ.

4. Discuss all or any of these fruit and their definitions. Share any thoughts, questions, struggles, and stories to process and better understand them.

   LOVE—caring from the soul of Jesus.

   JOY—feeling from the heart of Jesus.

   PEACE—having the mind of Jesus.

   PATIENCE—waiting quietly on God's timing.

   KINDNESS—showing the love of Jesus.

   GOODNESS—having the motives of Jesus.

FAITHFULNESS—expressing the loyalty of Jesus.

GENTLENESS—having the character of Christ.

SELF-CONTROL—surrendering your will to God's power

5. Share the fruit that you feel you are strongest in and then the one you feel is your weakest. Explain.

(This week has fewer questions to allow plenty of time to discuss the fruit of the Spirit in question 4.)

> **POST/TWEET**
>
> If we do the right thing in the wrong way, people can miss the right thing that we do. #stopwatchingstartdoing

CHAPTER 10

WILL YOU START DOING?

JOAN OF ARC

It was the summer in France and Joan, 13, was working around noon in her father's garden when she reported seeing a bright light and hearing a voice. It told her to "live a virtuous life." The Voice began to come more frequently, until one day she was told that she would save France. Joan questioned the Voice and asked how she could possibly accomplish this! The Voice answered, "God will be with you." (Sound familiar from another young lady in the Bible who asked how God could possibly do what the angel said?)

After nine months of relentless attempts, she managed to convince the authorities that she was sent by God to save France. She rode over 300 miles on horseback through enemy territory with a banner of knights to the dauphin, Charles, with the message that he should be crowned the rightful king.

He turned her over to the church. She was questioned for weeks, but the counsel finally reported "only humility, purity, honesty, and simplicity" in regards to Joan. She rode out again and led 4,000 troops to take back the city of Orleans. In the battle of Les Tourelles, she was struck through the shoulder with an arrow. It was removed and Joan returned to the fight, which inspired the French army to force the English army into retreat. After the recapture of the town of Reims, the dauphin was finally crowned king, but he would not drive the English out of Paris. Within the year, Joan, now 18, was captured by France's enemy. She was placed in prison for months and charged with 70 counts of heresy. She troubled the church by claiming divine revelation, prophesying the future, and claiming that her eternal salvation was secure. Joan claimed accountability to God first and the church second.

Finally, Joan was released to the government and on May 30, 1431 at 9:00 a.m., Joan, now 19, walked toward the market square for public execution. She knelt down and prayed for her enemies, then stood at the pyre—a pre-prepared bonfire for burning a person alive. As the flames shot up around her, she fixed her eyes on a cross she had requested to be mounted above her. Her final word was recorded as ... "Jesus."

One of her most famous quotes to the authorities who questioned her: "If I were to say that God sent me, I shall be condemned, but God really did send me." 25 years after her execution, a church commission overturned her charges and declared her innocent. In 1920, the Roman Catholic Church canonized Joan as a saint.

EVERETT SWANSON/COMPASSION INTERNATIONAL

In 1952, evangelist Everett Swanson (no relation to author EJ) went to South Korea to preach the Gospel to troops in the Republic of Korea's army. During his visit, he was moved by the number of orphaned children left by the war. In a discussion about this issue, a missionary challenged Reverend Swanson, "You have seen the tremendous needs and unparalleled opportunities of this land. What do you intend to do about it?"

In effect, this missionary was saying, "Are you going to keep watching or start doing?" Or maybe a better paraphrase would be, "Are you going to go back home and ignore what you've seen or help these children?"

Swanson returned to the United States and, along with his wife, Miriam, and the help of Dr. Gus and Helen Hemwall, a ministry was launched on behalf of these orphans. Reverend Swanson began to share about the needs of the Korean children at his revival meetings. Christians began to donate funds to purchase food, medical care, and basic living needs. By 1954, the sponsorship program that Compassion still uses today was born, whereby people could help a specific child by giving a monthly gift. Children were provided food, shelter, medical care, and Bible instruction.

In 1963, Swanson was becoming uneasy about his name being the focus of this growing ministry. He was inspired by Jesus' words in Matthew 15:32: "I have compassion on the multitude. I will not send them away hungry." So, the ministry name was changed and is now known worldwide as Compassion International. What begun as a missionary's challenge to start doing is now a vital ministry in 26 countries, serving 1.2 million children—and growing.

Thank God that Everett Swanson decided to do something. Over 1 million children are certainly glad he did.

For more info, go to Compassion.com.

WILLIAM BOOTH & THE SALVATION ARMY

In the mid-1860s, William Booth was preaching the Gospel to criminals, prostitutes, gamblers, and drunkards in the slums of London. When the people would respond and accept Christ, he tried to connect them to local churches, but the leaders wouldn't allow them in. So Booth started a small army of newly converted believers who sang hymns and preached in the streets with him. It was a growing, living, powerful testimony of the redemption and grace of God. Not hidden in the walls of a church, but alive and available on the streets.

By 1874, Booth had 1,000 volunteers and 42 evangelists serving under the name "The Christian Mission" and his disciples had started calling him "General." When he was proofing a report on the ministry, he saw the words "volunteer army" and he crossed out "volunteer" and wrote the word "Salvation." In August of 1878, the Salvation Army was born.

WILL YOU START DOING?

The first meeting held in America was in Philadelphia in 1879. In 1880, General Booth sent eight Salvationists to begin a full-time work in the U.S. Booth died in 1912, but his vision and passion live on in over 100 countries. So, the next Christmastime when you see the red bucket in front of the mall and hear the ringing bell, think about the man who started doing street ministry in the slums of London and reaching "the least of these."

For more info, go to Salvationarmyusa.org

ZACH HUNTER & LOOSE CHANGE TO LOOSEN CHAINS

At 12 years old, Zach Hunter found out that slavery was still prevalent. He says, "I was really surprised to find out that there are over 27 million slaves in the world today. I had all these emotions about it and I wasn't sure what to think about the idea of modern slavery. But I didn't think it was enough to just have emotions."

So Zach started doing. He launched "Loose Change to Loosen Chains." The idea is that young people solicit and collect people's loose change and then give it to organizations that work toward ending slavery, both through actual intervention and also education on the issue.

Zach has written three books to date: *Be the Change, Generation Change*, and *Lose Your Cool*. He also speaks to audiences all over the world. Zach has inspired his generation to dedicate their lives to Christ and allow Him to use them to solve the problems of the world—not just slavery, but whatever God leads them to.

For more info, go to Zachhunter.me.

KATIE DAVIS & AMAZIMA MINISTRIES

In December of 2006, 18-year-old Katie Davis from Brentwood, Tennessee, traveled to Uganda for the first time. Something eternal happened to her there.

In the summer of 2007, Katie went back to Uganda to teach Kindergarten at an orphanage. She was surprised by the number of children sitting on the side of the road or out working in the fields. There were no government-run public schools in the area of Uganda where she was living. Most schools are privately operated and require fees for attendance, making most children unable to afford an education.

Katie began a child sponsorship program matching orphaned children with sponsors. A gift of $300 provides for one child to go to school, school supplies, daily hot meals, spiritual discipleship, and medical care. By January of 2008, Katie had signed up 150 kids into the program. To date, the program sponsors over 600 children.

Katie established a non-profit organization called Amazima Ministries International that seeks to meet the physical, emotional, and spiritual needs of orphaned children in Uganda. In the Lugandan language, Amazima means "truth."

She also started a feeding program to the Karimojong community with over 1,200 children being fed Monday through Friday. This allows the children to attend school and keep off the streets, also providing medical care, Bible study, and health training.

Katie wanted to help the women in the village provide for their families, so she initiated a program for them to make Ugandan bead necklaces. The necklaces made by the Karimojong women are purchased and sold in the United States.

In January of 2008, Katie became the adopted mother of three orphaned girls. To date, now the mother of 13 daughters, she says, "People tell me I am brave. People tell me I am strong. People tell me 'good job.' Well, here is the truth of it. I am really not that brave, I am not really that strong, and I am not doing anything spectacular. I am just doing what God called me to do as a follower of Him. Feed His sheep, do unto the least of His people."

For more info, go to Amazima.org.

THE BIRTH OF *I WON'T WATCH*

Here is a personal testimony from E.J. Swanson, one of the authors of this book...

"In 2011, I saw an ad for these fashion watches that MTV was selling. It said that 10 percent of each watch sale would go to a humanitarian organization. I immediately thought, '10 percent? I bet I could give away more than that! And the money could go to an organization where Christ is the focus.

"After some brainstorming with my wife, Abbey, and my friend, Ryan Smith, we came up with this idea of 'Stop Watching, Start Doing.' To challenge and inspire Christians to not just look at the many problems in our world, but to decide to take action.

"People ask, 'So why a watch?' The simple answer is people glance at their watch an average of 20 times a day. So 20 times a day, the *I Won't Watch* can remind people to keep making a difference in the world in the name of Christ.

"People also ask, 'You thought you could do better than 10 percent. How'd that go?' Well, we give away an average of $10 per item sold, and as much as $13, 40–50 percent of each sale.

"To date, millions of dollars have been given to ministries such as Compassion International, Charity Water, To Write Love on Her Arms, Living Water International, NURU, Not for Sale, International Justice Mission, and CURE International. These watches have provided meals for hungry children, medical screenings to help prevent diseases, and shelter to girls at risk of falling victim to the sex trade, just to name a few.

"The inspiration for this book came from fellow Christ-followers such as Everett Swanson, William Booth, and Zach Hunter, but the title concept came from the *I Won't Watch* movement. You can join #thewatchrevolt at Iwontwatch.com."

BY FAITH, I . . .

In Hebrews 11, we see this continuing, repeated phrase: "By faith . . . "

By faith, Abel . . .

By faith, Enoch . . .

By faith, Noah . . .

By faith, Abraham . . .

By faith, Isaac . . .

By faith, Jacob . . .

By faith, Joseph . . .

By faith, Moses . . .

By faith, Rahab . . .

By faith, Gideon . . .

By faith, Barak . . .

By faith, Samson . . .

By faith, Jephthah . . .

By faith, David . . .

By faith, Samuel . . .

By faith, the Prophets . . .

Now listen to the conclusion of this chapter, verses 39–40 . . .

> *All of them pleased God because of their faith! But still they died without being given what had been promised. This was because God had something better in store for us. And he did not want them to reach the goal of their faith without us.* (CEV)

Did you see it?! . . . "without us." That's you and me. God wants you to be added to this list—this Hall of Fame of His followers of faith.

In the space below, write in your first name.

By faith, _____

Next, write on the lines below what you would want God to write about you. Dream big! Step out in your faith! What would like to be written about you? By your faith in Christ, what do you want to be true about your life?

_____
_____
_____
_____
_____

Place this message and prayer, from your own heart to God, somewhere where you can see it frequently, so that in the days, months, and years ahead you can remind yourself of your true goal in life.

JESUS

The stories and testimonies from this chapter of ordinary people who did extraordinary acts are our final inspiration before you launch out into the world with your own gift and passion. To create your own story that someone will write of, others will speak of, of yet another ordinary person who showed amazing courage and accomplished extraordinary acts to glorify a Mighty God!

Let's look at one more, one final unique life story written by Dr. James Allan Francis in 1926.

"He was born in an obscure village, the child of a peasant woman. He grew up in still another village, where He worked in a carpenter shop until He was 30. Then for three years He was an itinerant preacher. He never wrote a book. He never held an office. He never had a family or owned a house. He didn't go to college. He never traveled more than 200 miles from the place He was born. He did none of the things one usually associates with greatness. He had no credentials. He was only 33 when public opinion turned against Him. His friends deserted Him. He was turned over to His enemies and went through the mockery of a trial. He was nailed to a cross between two thieves. When He was dying, His executioners gambled for His clothing, the only property He had on earth. When He was dead, He was laid in a borrowed grave through the pity of a friend. Nineteen centuries have come and gone and today He is the central figure of the human race, the leader of mankind's progress. All the armies that ever marched, all the navies that ever sailed, all the parliaments that ever sat, all the kings that ever reigned, put together, have not affected the life of man on earth as much as that One Solitary Life. Do You Know Who He Is?"

The true and lasting motivation for someone to stop watching and start doing is not to do humanitarian works or even to change the world. The real motivation is because Jesus gave His life, so that we might live. We serve a Risen Savior and we owe Him our very lives. It is important to save souls and to heal the hurting and —yes, change the world—but only because of Jesus and what He has done. No other reason. No other motive.

> *Then I saw in the right hand of him who sat on the throne a scroll with writing on both sides and sealed with seven seals. And I saw a mighty angel proclaiming in a loud voice, "Who is worthy to break the seals and open the scroll?" But no one in heaven or on earth or under the earth could open the scroll or even look inside it. I wept and wept because no one was found who was worthy to open the scroll or look inside. Then one of the elders said to me, "Do not weep! See, the Lion of the tribe of Judah, the Root of David, has triumphed. He is able to open the scroll and its seven seals." Then I saw a Lamb, look-*

ing as if it had been slain, standing in the center of the throne, encircled by the four living creatures and the elders. He had seven horns and seven eyes, which are the seven spirits of God sent out into all the earth. He came and took the scroll from the right hand of him who sat on the throne. And when he had taken it, the four living creatures and the twenty-four elders fell down before the Lamb. Each one had a harp and they were holding golden bowls full of incense, which are the prayers of the saints. And they sang a new song: "You are worthy to take the scroll and to open its seals, because you were slain, and with your blood you purchased men for God from every tribe and language and people and nation. You have made them to be a kingdom and priests to serve our God, and they will reign on the earth." Then I looked and heard the voice of many angels, numbering thousands upon thousands, and ten thousand times ten thousand. They encircled the throne and the living creatures and the elders. In a loud voice they sang: "Worthy is the Lamb, who was slain, to receive power and wealth and wisdom and strength and honor and glory and praise!" Then I heard every creature in heaven and on earth and under the earth and on the sea, and all that is in them, singing: "To him who sits on the throne and to the Lamb be praise and honor and glory and power, for ever and ever!" (Revelation 5:1–12, NIV)

Do you sense the awe around these verses? The sheer majesty and power of Christ as the Savior of the world, the Only One Who could do anything about our sin? Living for Him is what this book is all about. Giving our lives to the One Who saved the world and is still saving it. And asks us to help Him! ... Wow!

Now God has us where he wants us, with all the time in this world and the next to shower grace and kindness upon us in Christ Jesus. Saving is all his idea, and all his work. All we do is trust him enough to let him do it. It's God's gift from start to finish! We don't play the major role. If we did, we'd probably go around bragging that we'd done the whole thing! No, we neither make nor save ourselves. God does both the making and saving. He creates each of us by Christ Jesus to join him in the work he does, the good work he has gotten ready for us to do, work we had better be doing. (Ephesians 2:7–10, MSG)

Notice the final phrase: "work we had better be doing."

Our prayer for you as you finish this book is that:

You know your gift or gifts.

You know your talents.

You understand why you've been given them.

You now know why you're on the earth.

You're going to use the rest of your life to serve Jesus Christ with all your heart, all your soul, all your mind, and all your strength.

You'll stand before your Heavenly Father one day and hear Him say, "Well done, good and faithful servant. Enter my Kingdom!"

We close with the same challenge the missionary gave to Reverend Swanson: "You have seen the tremendous needs and unparalleled opportunities [that God has shown you]. What do you intend to do with it?"

It's time to . . . Stop Watching and Start Doing!

CHAPTER 10 DISCUSSION QUESTION

For your final discussion time for this book, there's just one directive: Talk about how you can carry out what God has placed on your heart for your own life.

> **POST/TWEET**
>
> Post/tweet your "By Faith" line, followed by hashtag #stopwatchingstartdoing.

BRING E.J. SWANSON TO YOUR CHURCH!

E.J. IS AVAILABLE TO SPEAK FOR:

- CHURCH SERVICES
- CHURCH SPECIAL EMPHASIS DAYS SUCH AS MISSIONS OR WORLD HUNGER
- STUDENT MINISTRY RALLIES
- STUDENT MINISTRY CAMPS
- STUDENT MINISTRY DISCIPLE NOW'S
- CHRISTIAN SCHOOL EVENTS
- DENOMINATION OR PARA-CHURCH CONFERENCES

GO TO EJSWANSON.ORG FOR MORE INFO AND BOOKING REQUEST FORM.

SCAN THIS QR CODE TO LAUNCH E.J.'S CONTACT PAGE.

JOIN E.J. IN FIGHTING GLOBAL POVERTY THROUGH I WON'T WATCH!

I Won't Watch was founded by E.J. Swanson in 2011 for the purpose of providing opportunities for people to combat the causes and conditions of poverty through the global sponsorship of water, shelter, education, and health initiatives.

FOR MORE INFO AND HOW YOU CAN BECOME A MEMBER OF THE WATCH REVOLT, GO TO IWONTWATCH.COM OR SCAN THE QR CODE.